"Hilary Kramer has championed the underdog investor for her entire long career as an investment guru and author. So her new book is must reading for anyone looking for an edge to make money in the market. Kramer's book is a must-read because she reveals not just where science, technology, and industry are heading, but how the everyday investor can use this knowledge to create wealth. Always entertaining and smart, Kramer can be counted on to cut through the mysteries of investing. The pros aren't going to like you knowing what Hilary is going to tell you."

—**JOHN CRUDELE**, syndicated columnist and business journalist, *New York Post*

"Hilary Kramer's sweet financial insight into making money from tomorrow's biggest concepts is as amazing as Ol' Blue Eyes teaming up with Sammy Cahn. Scoobey, doobey, doo... She's packed this book with cutting-edge 'GameChangers' that will turbocharge your own portfolio. If you haven't heard of digital bullion... echo moms... cold chain logistics... acquatic superfoods... MindWars, you will! Kramer's talent is making these opportunities understandable and actionable for the everyday investor in a way that gives you the same long-term advantages as the professionals. This book is right on the money and is gonna be big, like Sinatra in Vegas big, baby!"

—**JOE PISCOPO**, actor, comedian, and radio talk show host, *The Joe Piscopo Morning Show* on the Salem Radio Network, AM970 The Answer

"Who wants to be a millionaire? Step one: Read Hilary Kramer's blockbuster *GameChanger Investing*. There is no more reliable and trusted voice for financial common sense in America than Hilary, and this book lays out the formula in simple, plain English."

—**STEPHEN MOORE**, senior economic advisor to Donald Trump and former *Wall Street Journal* editorial board member

"*GameChanger Investing* is an engaging and insightful vision of the future. Kramer has produced a thorough investigation of break-throughs about to emerge in the world of computing, communications, consumption, and health care. Anyone interested in profiting from the coming tsunami of global change will learn a lot from this book and be entertained along the way."

—**JON D. MARKMAN**, *Forbes* columnist and author of *Fast Forward Investing*

"What will determine your success as an investor in coming years? Hilary Kramer, Wall Street's one-woman research powerhouse, says it's the ability to identify and invest in winning trends. Her new book peels back the research that the smart money is using to pull in monster profits in the next decade. Kramer opens a window on the advances in artificial intelligence, bionics for longevity, mobility, geospatial data, blockchain technology, and how investors must understand these innovations and disruptors to build wealth. All other investing is like driving while looking in the rearview mirror—a surefire way to crash rather than win the game of investing for the big bucks."

—**MARK STUART GILL**, contributing writer, *Bottom Line Personal*

"In these tumultuous times, we all need a plan, and with *GameChanger Investing*, Hilary Kramer charts about as clear a course as one can find these days. The book is a cogent and pre-scient look at the trends that will be shaping our lives and the lives of our children in the coming decades, and how savvy investors can capitalize on them. Hilary Kramer, with her legendary, well-earned reputation as a futurist and visionary investor, tells the reader how to cash in on the billions coming down the pike from all this global change."

—**SCOTT NORVELL**, former international bureau chief and vice president, Fox News Channel

"Hilary Kramer is setting the world on fire. She is really smart and extremely insightful. You can't go wrong following her advice."

—**PHIL BOYCE**, senior vice president of Salem Radio Network

"Hilary Kramer has had years of success in her *GameChangers* newsletter identifying stocks that are truly changing the way we live our lives—making her subscribers a ton of money along the way. Now she's sharing her secrets and the insights she's learned over the years with everyone. Read this book and I promise you that you'll be a better investor and have a head start on everyone else concerning the next set of trends that will make investors millions."

—**ROGER MICHALSKI**, vice president/group publisher, Eagle Financial Publications

"There's a new Kramer in town, and her new book is the next *Megatrends*. It's appropriate that her book is being published in 2020, as she has laser-like, 20/20 vision in predicting the future in science, tech, and geopolitics. Her book not only updates you on all the creative disruption going on in robotics, the Internet of Things, cryptocurrencies, self-driving cars, artificial intelligence, genetic and medical breakthroughs, space travel, online retail, and job markets, but gives you solid advice at the end of each chapter on how to profit from each trend. I've never seen a better quick survey for investors."

—**DR. MARK SKOUSEN**, presidential fellow, Chapman University, and editor of *Forecasts & Strategies*

GameChanger Investing

GameChanger Investing

HOW TO PROFIT FROM TOMORROW'S BILLION-DOLLAR TRENDS

HILARY KRAMER

NATIONALLY SYNDICATED HOST OF
KRAMER'S MILLIONAIRE MAKER

REGNERY
CAPITAL

Regnery Capital™ is a trademark of Salem Communications Holding Corporation
Regnery® is a registered trademark of Salem Communications Holding Corporation

Cataloging-in-Publication data on file with the Library of Congress

ISBN 978-1-68451-005-4
ebook ISBN 978-1-68451-023-8

Published in the United States by
Regnery Capital
An imprint of Regnery Publishing
A Division of Salem Media Group
300 New Jersey Ave NW
Washington, DC 20001
www.Regnery.com

Manufactured in the United States of America

10 9 8 7 6 5 4 3 2 1

Books are available in quantity for promotional or premium use. For information on discounts and terms, please visit our website: www.Regnery.com.

For Shia and Timmy

Contents

Embrace the Future and Invest in Tomorrow's GameChanging Billion-Dollar Trends

Look how far we've come. When I was young, we were turning the television channels manually—all seven of them—and we waited for our weekly *TV Guide* to arrive in the mailbox so we could plan our schedule around our beloved shows. Back then, ABC's *Wide World of Sports* let us share each week in "the thrill of victory and the agony of defeat." As much as TV and everything else in our world have changed, that phrase still strikes a chord. In investing, as in sports, there are winners and losers. My job is to help make sure you enjoy the thrill of victory —and avoid the agony of defeat. The secret? Opening a window into the future, showing you how to be a GameChanger Investor by capturing the enormous rewards just beyond tomorrow.

I see plenty of room for prosperity in the future. I can afford to be confident for a simple reason: In my career on Wall Street and then as an independent global wealth manager and venture capitalist, I've seen the best outcomes that human innovation can produce. These inventions and advances have created wealth beyond imagination and allowed individual investors—even with limited funds—to become millionaires. The future is limitless, and you can make an immense fortune by seizing

the GameChanging trends ahead. As you will read in the pages that follow, GameChanger Investing requires vision. We're not looking for
companies that are already priced like giants with a spectacular future
to match. My goal is to find companies with spectacular futures that are
priced like the start-ups they are.

Wall Street seems short on vision these days. Even the smartest investors operate within closer and closer horizons. Portfolios that were once
painstakingly designed to mature over generations are now reeling from
market spasms that play out over weeks, days, or even hours. We live in
a world where trading technology can build fortunes in microseconds
and flash crashes can wipe out everyone faster than you can count.

People no longer plan beyond the next quarterly earnings cycle.
They're living day to day, moment to moment. That's no way to live, and
frankly it's no way to invest. That's why I wrote this book. Through
endless market twists, turns, and turmoil, as long as people keep innovating, dreaming, and executing, great companies grow and create wealth.
You can be one of those investors who cashes in by following the
"GameChangers."

I will identify the GameChanging trends that will shape your investment decisions and expand your financial goals exponentially. Those
trends are happening all around us. For example, increasingly sophisticated business and engineering processes are now being run on mobile
devices, transforming our relationship to time, information, and the
difference between work and play. The average smartphone has about a
million times more computing power than the computers that put a man
on the Moon, and 2.7 times what a top-of-the-line supercomputer could
boast just thirty years ago. We all carry the world's library in our pockets, but that's just one aspect of the transformation that is taking place.

In my three decades in the inner sanctum of Wall Street, you'd
think I'd have seen it all. But the trends, sectors, and companies we will
talk about here surprise and thrill me every day. I will take you where
the action is. To borrow a phrase from a classic book, these are the
"megatrends" of tomorrow. These are the technologies, demographic
factors, and cultural currents that are changing the world. Let's imagine

the world of tomorrow together and invest our capital and attention accordingly so we can capture the affluence which time and change will unlock. Leave the quarter-to-quarter worrying to investors with no vision. This is where we can beat the high-speed trading firms, who only think milliseconds ahead. When the bell rings five years from now, you'll come out ahead as long as you keep your eyes on the road and never let them get stuck on the rear-view mirror. As we get started, I want you to keep three things in mind.

1. "Technology" is out of the bag now.

It wasn't that long ago that Apple and Microsoft were GameChanging concepts taking shape in their founders' garages. Yet today, computing devices running their software are in billions of hands, and the companies that were once fledgling IPOs are now trillion-dollar pillars of the global economy.

Steve Jobs, Bill Gates, and their countless collaborators and competitors launched a digital revolution that hasn't ended. When they started, computers were slow, massive, and prohibitively expensive tools that only the largest organizations and governments could afford or even train people to program. The notion that an individual might own one was outlandish.

A generation later, the world is covered with devices that have the power to beat a chess master or pilot a rocket to the Moon. They're learning how to drive cars, operate factories, and perform surgery. And that's only what's coming over the next horizon as every generation of chips gets smaller, faster, and cheaper.

But people in Silicon Valley get lost in the silicon world. Every company in the technology sector is built on smart forms of sand that can transmit and store information. Their world is still just billions of semiconductors talking to each other.

The real technological revolution of tomorrow brings the microchips back into the real world. It's not about building faster chips but finding new ways to work with them, programming them to support the lives we want to lead. Tomorrow's technology companies run in the background, driving complex business processes as well as smart cars. They can do the work of organs and limbs lost to accident, disease, or old age. They teach and entertain, transmitting age-old messages alongside the latest headlines.

They won't replace human beings. How could they? They can augment the human experience and liberate us from the tasks that a modern computer can truly do better, but we're a long way from robots that can dance, mourn, pray, or fall in love. Even the finest artificial intelligence can only respond to events that match the patterns in its memory. It can't improvise well, and it can't plan a better future.

Technology has no ambition. The world's computers are all just slightly more sophisticated hammers and knitting needles, tools waiting to be deployed to fit some human purpose. It's up to us to decide how to deploy all this power. We pick the apps on our phones, and while we can teach them to suggest whom we should call at a scheduled time, we're still the ones doing all the talking.

And in the final analysis, that interaction between tools and users is where "technology" really happens. The thrill was only briefly in the competition for the best silicon chips. Now it's in building bridges between Silicon Valley and the real world. As the chips become ubiquitous, money is free to flow in different directions.

Consider a lot of the stocks we've been trained to consider "technology" companies. Amazon got its start as a pioneering dot-com marketplace, but now that every store has an online presence and most at least consider home delivery, Amazon's website no longer makes it special. Jeff Bezos's behemoth is now just another consumer discretionary company. It's just another store.

Admittedly, Amazon is one of the biggest stores in the world, and it's still growing as fast as it can, but it is no longer fundamentally different from Walmart or Target or Costco. Those companies all have computers, websites, and home delivery. While Bezos may still have slightly better computers, pure digital power is no longer the all-or-nothing competitive barrier it once was. The "technology" has already been incorporated into the way his company operates in the modern world. He's running a big store.

Likewise, Alphabet (Google) is a lot more than a search engine now, and Facebook has matured since the days when it was just the site people checked to keep up with college friends. Just as the telephone once gave us a way to talk at a distance, we now use the infrastructure these companies have built to support an endless conversation that can go around the planet. And since access is free and theoretically ubiquitous—you can log in anywhere—these aren't really "technology" pioneers now either. Their core business is communications, moving ideas around. They're classed with the phone companies, cable network carriers, television channels, and old-fashioned print publishers.

Even Apple is no longer a "tech" company. While it's still formally a technology stock, the giant of Cupertino has been more a consumer device manufacturer ever since the original iPod changed the company's fortunes. Its real competitors are companies that make home audio equipment, headphones, televisions, fitness monitors, and telephones. Eventually, it might start building its own cars as well. Apple devices are a lot smarter than those that previous generations grew up with, but the computers themselves are now just a small piece of the overall calculation here.

Apple, however, is also an entertainment company, selling access to music, books, and videos. It is a financial services company thanks to Apple Pay and the Apple Card. And the App Store is the biggest software marketplace in the world. Any of these businesses would qualify for membership in various market sectors, but the sum of the parts is unique.

All four of these giant companies are disrupting the settled commercial landscape in endless ways, big and small, but the real innovators on my screen were never computer makers. They are unlikely to ever cause upheavals in Silicon Valley. The days of Silicon Valley disruption as a goal in itself are over. If you love data for their own sake, that's great. There's still plenty in this book for you! But recognize that the future that interests me—and where I see the real investment opportunities—is out there in the world that intersects with Silicon Valley.

PayPal and Square are not officially technology stocks. Their payment systems are changing the way money circulates in exchange for goods and services, but the computers remain deep in the background. Wherever kids pass a few digital dollars from phone to phone to pay the small debts they rack up with each other, these companies are in the background.

As far as those kids are concerned, nothing dramatic or even noteworthy is happening. They don't see anything strange about purchasing power beaming back and forth without ever turning into physical currency. It's just another form of data, points in a video game. Arguably that's all money ever was, first when it was precious metals and then numbers on paper. The only difference now is how fast it moves and the ways it can accumulate.

Kids in the future will grow up with a dramatically different relationship to what we consider cutting-edge technology today. Just as we learned to change TV channels (sometimes without even using a remote) and heat food in the microwave, they're already interacting with a new generation of devices and the data flowing around and between them. We don't call a microwave high technology. They won't even pause to think that it's unusual to ask the refrigerator to order its own milk.

Just like that refrigerator manufacturer of tomorrow, most of the companies we'll investigate in the following pages will make their mark on everyday life. Despite the fortunes that have been accumulated in Silicon Valley in recent decades, the real world is always where the biggest economic transformations take place. So leave your computer jargon at the door. If it can't be explained in plain language to folks who don't know a thing about the inner workings of computers, it's all just chatter.

And there's another fact that we should all digest as we look toward the world of 2050 and beyond…

2. The future isn't evenly distributed (yet).

That phrase from a William Gibson science fiction novel has never been true like it is today. Some parts of the world are already approaching

2050 on a clear glide path. Others are still digesting the innovations of the past few decades as they catch up fast.

Never forget that while 2.4 billion people log into Facebook every month, another 4 billion don't have reliable Internet access at all. The good news is that they're coming online fast, usually as smart phone prices drop to where nearly everyone can afford a connection. Over the next five years, companies like Facebook will have another 2 billion potential subscribers around the world, and by 2050 all but a few remote corners of the globe will be wired into the network.

These are big numbers that boil down to a simple truth: The first wave of Internet adoption in the West is mature now, but the global market opportunity is still growing at 10 percent a year and shall be for the foreseeable future. That's 400 million people hitting the information superhighway for the first time every twelve months—more people than live in North America today.

Some of these people come from communities which haven't changed much in centuries. Standards of living are low; things we take for granted, like a varied diet and clean clothes, don't exist, let alone broadband streaming video. When these hundreds of millions of people start interacting online with the rest of the world, a whole lot of human potential will be unleashed for the first time in history.

Think of the power of China's long transformation from agrarian economy to modern industrial powerhouse, taking one billion people all the way from village life to the global metropolis in barely a generation. They didn't bother building a lot of stores in many of China's new cities because people shop online. They didn't buy a lot of computers, televisions, or fixed-line cable networks either because the overwhelming majority of these people skipped those intermediate stages. They went straight to the 4G phone. That's their mall, their bank, their stereo system, and living room entertainment screen.

In a lot of ways, what China and other emerging economies need from the digital world renders everything else irrelevant. Think of these billions of people as the children of tomorrow, the mainstream market of 2050. To the extent that their tastes and ambitions line up with those of Western kids, I think they'll drive the future in roughly the same direction.

After all, the biggest movies every year are the same on both sides of the Pacific Ocean. They know the Beatles in China, and they have Elvis impersonators. There's a Disneyland in Shanghai and another in Hong Kong. As India, Indonesia, and other countries join the global media ecosystem, we'll see even greater convergence of narratives, beloved characters, and the shared cultural experiences that make long distance friendship possible.

Companies that can operate on all sides of this ecosystem can make a lot of money by exporting American media to billions of eager consumers and bringing back the biggest fads from overseas. Think of the craze when the Beatles first came to America. Multiply it exponentially. Along with fads come products, merchandising, fashion, and accessories.

And we're not just talking about entertainment. Work moves back and forth across the planet now as corporate employers chase human resources wherever they're willing to accept a competitive wage, and employees realize that one can live anywhere and phone in the results of every productive working day. The telecommuting dream is becoming the status quo. "Virtual" jobs blur the line between offshore and onshore hiring. When the "office" is a construct of the computing cloud, people from everywhere can collaborate across state lines, national borders, and time zones.

More information accessible on demand and more people to ponder it practically guarantee that the rate of scientific progress will accelerate. Processes are fast-tracked as the obstacles of distance and intermediation fall back in the face of continuous data. Once upon a time, if documents needed to be verified, a lag of several weeks was normal due to shipping time. Sometimes those documents were lost, and the process had to be repeated. Not anymore.

Similarly, it took days to execute a single stock trade. Quarterly dividends and other investor rewards were distributed as paper checks in the mail, which in turn needed to be brought to a physical bank, deposited, and processed before the money could be used. Checks denominated in foreign currency took even longer to work their way through the system. Now it's almost instantaneous.

Once again, the companies making all this happen have a vast task ahead of them, which makes them interesting to investors like us, who want to capture the leaders of tomorrow at today's valuations. They're building a lot of virtual "real estate" that will put them in a position to charge the equivalent of rent (or at least tolls) in the new economy that emerges. The quickest way to connect the world would be to broadcast 5G technologies worldwide using a fleet of self-powered drones and balloons that hover twenty to fifty kilometers above the earth. Mankind's collective intelligence is ever expanding and changing the way people relate across cultures and throughout the business world. We're going to need all of that bandwidth. But that's a story for later in this book.

For now, the lesson I want you to take from this discussion is that the Internet boom is far from over. Even by the least optimistic estimates, we're only 50 percent of the way to wiring the world, which means that the companies which led the way in the first wave can double their business before running out of opportunities—and upstarts that find ways to do it better can grow to the size of today's giants.

It's going to be a decades-long process either way, with false starts, reversals, and a lot of slow but steady progress. People around the world will keep joining the global conversation, bringing new points of view, new concerns, and plenty of fresh ideas. Concerns mean opportunities. Ideas provide solutions.

3. The future is always uncertain (and that's a good thing).

The world can seem dangerously unsteady today. There's no system for delegating authority or supporting world-class expertise. Sometimes it feels like nobody is in charge. That's not a bad thing in itself, but it is a very different world from my parents'. It's more democratic, and there are more risks and rewards associated with picking one direction and sticking with it. Someone with ambition, a strong work ethic, and a little luck can go further in this kind of world because there are fewer barriers to hold him back. There's a more level playing field—in some ways absolutely level—with no barriers to competing in the free market.

This is a Twitter world where CEOs can communicate directly and instantaneously with customers, shareholders, and competitors, bypassing the old PR system that kept them apart. Even the White House communicates in real time without an institutional filter. We have a gig economy, a hustle economy. Uber makes the family car a revenue center. Airbnb does the same to the family home. If you've got the hustle, technology can help you monetize.

When I was just starting on Wall Street, the world was full of institutional barriers preventing any of that from happening. Companies went through excruciating procedures to sell stock on the public market. (I remember it all too well, having worked on a few IPOs in my day.) Yet despite the intricate and confusing regulations, individual investors were at the mercy of a nebulous world of stockbrokers, analysts, and other intermediaries doling out information and misinformation in equal measure. Good financial information was reserved for the people who paid the most. The rest of us had an extremely hard time finding out when a company was going to report its quarterly performance numbers, let alone knowing anything about "consensus" or whisper targets.

If anything, regulation ensured that tiny companies and the investors who focused on them lost the only advantage their size provided: flexibility. We couldn't be agile, hire or fire incremental part-time labor to meet demand. We couldn't scale as adroitly, and then, because compliance burdens were high, we couldn't scale as fast. And a lot of great companies got lost in the pecking order of investment banking client privilege, where big wheels paid a lot for preferential treatment and everyone else was almost entirely ignored.

The tax code now rewards entrepreneurial business. Technology ensures that every single-person shop has the same reach as a sprawling 300,000-person enterprise. If you're smart and open to the opportunities, you can outcompete the giant for the business you need to capture. Will you grow into a 300,000-person enterprise? Is that even your goal?

Admittedly, this is a riskier world for all of us. There are no safe lifetime jobs. You will have to reinvent yourself again and again. That's the price of our digital world. The future is entrepreneurial. The future is venture capital. The future is in GameChanger Investing.

We have no idea what the next president's favorite sectors will be, but we can see where technology and innovation is taking us. The future is up to us: private enterprise, open markets, we the people. Remember infrastructure back in 2017? Dead money. It was never "infrastructure week." Someone's going to rebuild, but it's not the federal government. Look to private companies and communities to step up.

Think the big banks are going to soar once the chains of regulation come off? They're already unchained. They have no idea what to do with their freedom. They're too big, sitting ducks, stalled battleships. Buy nimble little next-generation financial companies. Buy fintech. Buy disruptors. Buy the local banks and credit unions that aren't scared of changing up the business model.

Buy the companies that sell picks and shovels to the miners of the new economy. Business services. Outsourcing. Payroll processing. HR as a service. Marketing as a service. Commerce as a service. Buy any company that gives solo operators the power to pay as they go for essential business functions that the giants have whole departments to serve. Buy H&R Block. Business returns are the only future that a company has now.

Buy the insurers. Those stocks are loving this. Buy the most innovative pharma you can find and hang on. Buy wildcat shale. OPEC is dying. It's going to take oil prices higher before it disintegrates. We're a net energy exporter now. Buy liquid natural gas shipping.

Keep your eyes open. The real winner hasn't been born yet. When you see it, pounce. We live in a world of challenges waiting for solutions. Solutions will come. The future is more agile. Self-driving taxis will always be on the go, never parking. We love our cars, but car sales are going to drop like a rock and never recover, taking the need for steel and aluminum with them.

Reinvent the mall. Reinvent retirement. Reinvent education. Reinvent housing. Accept the risk of failure because you will fail often. There is no return without risk. The new era revives the appetite for risk. Dare to do great things, fully knowing that you might publicly fail. Take chances.

Mixing It Up with Volatility

The average age of the U.S. population is going to start going down soon. Millennials and their kids are coming up. Remember what it was like to be young as a nation. Take some calculated risks. Scramble some economic eggs. Gamble a little money. Maybe you'll lose, but with the right portfolio, you'll be winning too. Show some conviction. Even if you're old, you can play. Here's how.

How GameChanging Stocks Feed the Future-Focused Portfolio

Society is always changing under the influence of new ideas or the new application of old ones. New products absorb market share that once belonged to other companies, or they create entirely new markets, siphoning money away from established areas of the economy. Somebody is always building a better mousetrap. That's innovation at work.

Of course, the established mousetrap makers are vulnerable to this cycle because they're the ones who lose market share to make room for better, more efficient, or simply more exciting competitors. When their once comfortable world gets disrupted, they need to match the innovator or, ideally, come out with something better. The winners are the ones who convince us that they're doing the best job improving our lives.

Most people on Wall Street work extremely hard to anticipate change or at least stay out of its way. They're afraid of backing companies that will ultimately lose the race to innovation. At its core, my investment strategy is all about identifying disruptive trends early enough for individual shareholders to back winners and participate in the rewards. Instead of fighting economic disruption or pretending it doesn't exist, I see my role as getting disruption on your side.

The world is full of hopeful startups which have already managed to raise a little cash on the strength of a dream. The ones that excite me have already started to prove that their ideas are good enough to make an impact. They're already showing signs of becoming the strong, stable companies of tomorrow, with futures bright enough to outshine any market volatility.

How do I find them? A true GameChanging stock must start with strong fundamentals and be in a position to benefit from various macro trends—or as I also call them, catalysts. Our expectations are realistic and reasonable. We aren't allocating a single dollar to anyone whose idea hasn't generated any money or evidence that it will. While a few of those ideas will ultimately triumph, most will simply vanish or get absorbed into another company when they run out of cash.

Never forget—every company is its founder's dream. He thought he had a great idea and convinced other people to share it, but in the end at least 70 percent of start-ups fail. There's no shame in trying and failing. We just don't want to pour a lot of our money into failures without instituting some prudent checks to improve our odds.

Understanding Fundamentals

This term is thrown around quite often, but what does it really mean? "Fundamentals" are what make up the core story of a company. They tell me if a stock is a worthwhile investment or not. They generally include information such as earnings, revenue, assets, and liabilities, which we use to evaluate the tangible effect of the disruptive idea that drives a company. If there's no tangible effect, you're just throwing money at a dream.

The first thing I look for is *earnings*. To compensate shareholders, every company eventually needs to take in more cash than it spends.

Plenty of great organizations operate under the assumption that they'll change the world by distributing other people's money. They're called charities, and one of my goals here is to help you accumulate enough wealth so that you can comfortably give some away. Until that happens, however, I generally like to see positive profit expanding 10 percent or more year-over-year. I also want to see if quarterly sales are accelerating at a similar rate, both on an annual and quarterly basis.

Next on my list is *price-to-earnings (PE) ratios*. If you do any investment research on your own, it's probably at the top of your list, too. While it's a telling metric, it can also be trickier than it initially seems. At its most basic, PE will tell you if a stock is cheap or expensive compared with the market. Great companies can be too expensive to make money for us today. The S&P 500 currently has a PE ratio of around 18, so if a stock is well beneath that, it could hold substantial value. But a stock that comes in higher than that isn't necessarily a bad buy. That's why I drill deeper than the surface numbers. You can lose money just as easily with a value stock and make a lot of money with high-PE stocks— it's all a matter of when you buy the stock and how long you hold it.

Another factor I look for is whether a company has a growing *debt load*. This is a major red flag, but keep in mind that there is no magic formula to determine how much debt is healthy—it varies from industry to industry. I typically invest in firms with relatively low debt-to-equity ratios because they add stability. It's even better if a company has actively reduced its debt load in recent years. You'll see me call this out as a selling point in my recommendations since it often highlights a proactive management team.

Return on equity, known as ROE, is another key fundamental that I track. This comes in handy when I calculate how profitable a stock is against its competitors. In its most basic form, ROE tells me how much profit a company generates with the money its shareholders have put in. ROE is a great tool if you want to separate the money pits from the cash cows. Typically I want to see a 15 percent or greater return on equity year-over-year.

So there's your crash course in fundamentals! Now, let's talk about how I find catalyst-driven opportunities, which is where I've made more of my personal wealth than anywhere else.

Cashing in on Catalysts

The conditions that materially affect your investments can change frequently. The big ones are trends like those we discuss in this book. They have a life cycle of their own, speeding up or slowing down in response to what's going on in the company, society, and the world. These factors are catalysts. The list of potential catalysts is enormous.

We like to invest in companies that are speeding up. Maybe a new product announcement is coming that will blow away competitors, or maybe a corporate leadership change is moving a company in a better direction. Maybe a competitor just stumbled and now there's vulnerable market share ready to capture. Someone in Washington may decide to fight for policies that give some types of business a lift or force others to carry a heavier regulatory load. There are so many potential catalysts that it's impossible to list them all, but they can play crucial roles in how a stock performs.

I've made my own fortune spotting catalysts early and moving the money I had to make sure those disruptive events played out in my favor. I participated in the dot-com boom of the 1990s, remaining open to the most dynamic ideas of the era when the cash was flowing, and then, when it was clear who the ultimate winners would be, I put the profits to work in the next cycle of innovation.

Some of my biggest profits came from very simple observations. I noticed there was no television programming for Latinos in the United States. Univision, the only major Spanish-speaking channel, was an important cultural connection and entertainment medium that should have been commanding much higher advertising rates. (This is where my fundamental analysis came into play.)

I invested shortly after Univision's IPO in 1997 and sold in 2001 when I saw competition like Telemundo becoming a real threat. When I was selling, the world started buying. That's all right. Over those four years, the competitive landscape had already changed in our favor, creating a lot of wealth for investors who had their eyes open. And of course, I was in Apple early, back before the iPhone. But that was a long time ago.

Every Innovator Becomes the Incumbent

Innovation is the law of the Wall Street jungle. The companies that develop a competitive edge grow at an accelerated rate, rewarding the investors who backed future heavyweights early on. The companies that fail to keep up with the curve drift and eventually falter, sacrificing both market share and relevance.

For a generation, the information technology sector was the most concentrated innovation engine around. The personal computer revolution and then the Internet transformed the way we work, shop, communicate, and play. In the process, manufacturers and programmers became some of the richest people on the planet. Now, however, with billions of "smart" devices already in the field, the remaining sales opportunities are harder to capture. Margins have deteriorated to the point that major hardware makers are priced like consumer appliance companies, and if innovation doesn't step up, even world-class brands will feel the drag.

Disruption breeds a new status quo, and successful revolutionaries eventually become the establishment. For those of us who want to stay ahead of the changes, the Silicon Valley status quo just doesn't cut it anymore. As I said earlier, we're not looking for companies that are already priced like giants; we want companies with spectacular futures that are priced like start-ups. That way, when the disruption comes around, it plays out in our favor. Let's take a look at where a few of the disruptors of tomorrow—the real unicorns—are moving over the high-tech horizon and the potential opportunities they represent.

Avoid Chasing Someone Else's Unicorn

I can already hear some of you asking, "But what about Uber? Airbnb? Snapchat?" and I understand the questions. These are some of the biggest innovators dominating Wall Street chatter right now. But unless you're a venture capitalist, if a company is so far from turning its technology into a viable business that it takes years just to clear the IPO window, you're probably not going to want to stick around for five to seven years for the payoff.

To be honest, I'm not sure any of the companies I've just mentioned will ever be true portfolio-transforming wins for new investors. They've raised so much private money that they can build their businesses to relatively mature levels before they hit the public market.

Furthermore, to make the late-stage venture capitalists happy, they need to debut for substantially more than they were worth in the last funding round. Uber, for example, needed to go public as an $82 billion stock, practically what Ford and General Motors are worth put together. Since GM earns its valuation on roughly one hundred times the revenue base that Uber currently commands and is generally a profitable enterprise, Uber still has to grow into its valuation before any but speculators can take it seriously.

It's an open question whether there's even enough room in the automotive market for Uber to justify its price. Uber already captures 70 percent of all the money flowing through the pay-per-ride industry. To boost its revenue one hundred times and stand up to GM, it's going to need to crush all the companies fighting over the remaining 30 percent, and then expand the market itself by 9900 percent. That means signing up another ninety-nine customers for every one person currently using Uber cars. My math says there simply aren't enough people, and certainly not enough who are willing and able to pay to get driven around.

We faced this challenge in the dot-com days. A company with a strong growth curve is clearly disrupting its economic environment, but you can't extrapolate that curve into the future forever. Sooner or later, usually within a few years, that growth rate will flatten out as the disruptive idea either becomes the new status quo or attracts competitors convinced that they can do what you're doing better.

And sometimes the curve simply hits a hard wall. Americans generally eat one breakfast a day. If you're already serving 300 million breakfasts every morning, you've done extremely well, but you're also on the edge of running out of mouths to feed. Investors who project your historical growth rate beyond that point to justify a future stock price are just fooling themselves. The time to buy into that universal breakfast stock is early on, maybe when it's barely one-tenth or even one-twentieth of its current size. When it has already conquered the world, there's no place left to go.

The trends we discuss in this book, on the other hand, are a long way from becoming a universal breakfast. While a few early movers in each field have already started disrupting the way money moves through the global economy, the really deep social effects are still years or even decades down the road. That gives early movers room to grow.

It also gives the next generation of improvers a little time to let the early movers lay the initial groundwork for the truly dazzling industries of tomorrow. Today those companies are barely dreams, if they exist at all. The future is where they'll prove their worth and generate wealth.

CHAPTER ONE

DEMOGRAPHICS ON OUR SIDE: LOOKING PAST THE ECHO BOOM

The eighteen-year Baby Boom changed the American economy forever as the consumption patterns of 77 million people shaped the housing cycle, job market, and ultimately the entire retail landscape. Baby Boomer toys, clothes, music, and movies dominated the national psyche, producing whole industries and generating vast wealth for investors in the process.

And now that the Baby Boomers are retiring at the staggering rate of ten thousand per day, quite a few investors are trading the climax of that generation's lifecycle. But there's a lot more to the future than assisted-living real estate investment trusts (REITs) and advanced biotech therapies. While the Baby Boom has been playing out its second act, its younger children—the even bigger Echo Boom we call "millennials"—have been preparing to take the economic spotlight. This time, there are three million more boomers than the postwar generation brought to the stage.

The oldest of them are turning forty now. The youngest are still in college. While their childhood and adolescence were punctuated with deep recessions, they're finally looking to pursue their adult lives in a decent economic climate, get out of their parents' houses permanently, and launch their own households and families. If they find a way to make it work, we could be on the brink of a fresh economic boom like the one we saw when the Baby Boom started forming households.

And in the meantime, the demographic shift is already changing the way Americans work, communicate, shop, and relax. The center of gravity is moving toward the way the new generation thinks. As the old one retires, that process will accelerate. Either way, this is where the organic growth in the economy will emerge: companies that deliver products and services Echo Boomers crave will ride the demographic tailwind, while those that don't will struggle. This is where we'll make money in the future. It's going to be exciting.

According to a report published by Accenture, millennials spend roughly $1.4 trillion annually in the United States alone, accounting for 25 percent of total retail sales. Far from the economic fringe (despite what some people still like to think), that's actually the status quo. For our purposes, the millennials already run the world. The question investors need to wrestle with today is what kind of world they want to leave their children to inherit in 2050 and beyond.

Who Are the Digital Natives?

After years of hearing industry consultants pontificate about how much support the millennial generation needs in the workplace, it's been wonderful to see young workers finally prove that they're as motivated, independent, and productive as their older counterparts. They have energy and brains. I think the future is going to be in good hands.

They're still optimistic enough to see a better future and young enough to make it happen. In the meantime, their sheer demographic gravity ensures that their own shifting consumption habits shape the economy, much as Baby Boomer tastes shaped the postwar decades. It helps to think of the millennial boom as being roughly where the Baby Boomers were in the early 1970s: adults in their early prime, with jobs, a place to live, and either children or the prospect of having kids in the near future. They may have the tattoos to remind them of a summer following dot-com music festivals or a winter of Occupy Wall Street protests, but the pull of putting down roots is getting stronger for them now.

They're settling down. They're consuming at a record rate to catch up with where previous generations would have been—these are the first-time home buyers and young parents flooding back to the suburbs or filling their shopping carts with home décor and appliances.

Only they're not always pushing an actual shopping cart around a physical store. That's where the specialized investment opportunities start emerging. Remember, this generation grew up in an online world. They're not afraid to give a website their credit card number and wait for everything to arrive in the mail.

And of course the digital natives can't be away from their phone screens for long, so I don't expect companies tied into that universe to vanish any time soon. Even though Amazon has made access to books easier than at any time in history, they don't read books any more, but they absorb vast amounts of text-based information. Facebook is still a text-based medium, and it's the ubiquitous platform by which this generation communicates and receives news. It's how they talk to each other, whether they're texting around the dinner table or separated by continents.

Naturally they still have a lot to learn, much as the Baby Boomers were far from done with their lives in the early 1970s. There are opportunities for other generations to learn from them and even pass on a little of our discipline and experience. One way or another, we can invest across the generation gap and enrich each other.

Millennials grew up in a wired world. When they were younger, this was a matter of play: messaging, social media, and video games. As they move up the career ladder, it applies to online shopping. The days when everyone would pile in the station wagon and drive to the shopping mall are gone. In fact, 30 percent of millennials do not even plan on buying a car because of ride-sharing apps such as Uber and Lyft.

Instead of going to shopping malls and jumping over each other to get the best deals, consumers stay at home and buy from their mobile device. This development has had an enormous effect on brick-and-mortar stores.

As cable television has become expensive, millennials have moved away from the cable box ("cutting the cord") and toward companies such as Netflix and Hulu. In fact, 80 percent of them have a Netflix account. Nobody is twisting their arms to subscribe: it's as natural to them as fixed cable TV service was to their parents.

Millennials use social media for a variety of reasons, but it really boils down to ubiquity. They want to see what friends are talking about. The millennial population lives in fear of missing out ("FOMO," they say). Social media users are constantly on the lookout for interesting articles, something that entertains them, and even a way of finding out more information than they had seen on the news. In a recent study, 91 percent of millennials use Facebook, and 81 percent use YouTube. Twitter lags.

Around 86 percent of U.S. millennials own a smartphone. Advertisers are eager to colonize that little screen with branding messages, but it's a tricky proposition. Only 1 percent of U.S. millennials say they would trust a brand more because of an advertisement. A company that wants to win their loyalty will have to engage them on social media rather than talk to them through the television.

When they're not staring at a screen, they're at the gym. Millennials are the most health-conscious generation the world has seen. Brands such as Whole Foods and Lululemon are thriving from their desire to eat healthy and exercise on a regular basis. Big Tobacco is in trouble.

Multiple deep recessions have left the Echo Boom ambivalent about the job market and skeptical about long-term career commitments. Instead we see rapid movement when upward mobility beckons or the millennial loses interest. They move around the country chasing engaging jobs. The most popular cities include Raleigh, Minneapolis–Saint Paul,

Austin, Denver, Seattle, New York, San Jose, Boston, San Francisco, and Washington.

Millennials in their thirties, who graduated into the 2008 recession, have finally secured stable employment and are starting families. Look for the suburbs to become relevant again as a new generation makes its bid for the American Dream. These suburban towns have all the same amenities as big cities—yoga classes, health food stores, and short commutes to work. The service industry is about to explode.

Echo Moms Make Up for Lost Time

Before the 2008 crash scared the millennials (with good reason), the typical new American mom was twenty-five years old. Here we are, more than a decade later, and that average age of first childbirth has crept up to nearly thirty. These women aren't forgoing motherhood altogether. They want to have kids, and they're obviously doing it. They're just doing it later and later. I should know—I was a little older when I had my first child.

I waited because I wanted a career first. But many millennial moms didn't have a choice. The layoffs of 2008–2009 were so savage and so fast that these women (and to be fair, most millennial men) still have a touch of post-crash traumatic disorder.

Back in 2000, the feeling was that jobs come and go but talent rises to the top. It took years after 2008 for millennials, who were little more than kids at the time, to feel secure again. The feeling then was that jobs are scarce, so hang on and accept whatever they give you. Eat any amount of abuse because at least you're eating. You definitely don't want to go on a long maternity leave or even a vacation.

And people who got stuck in the temporary track may have longed for something more stable before they even thought about asking for maternity leave. Permanent temping (as opposed to temp-to-permanent, which is great) means never knowing where you're going to be in a year.

You can't plan a family or even put down roots because the job market can shift so much from year to year.

Women, who tended to be in relatively recession-resistant service and information industries and who made fewer demands, kept their jobs throughout the crash and post-crash. It's a stereotype but it's true: more women are single caregivers, and single caregivers think of the kids. I know a lot of women who stayed in terrible jobs over the past five years because they needed to put food on the table.

That's new. It used to be that women who worked were single girls waiting to get married, and they would give notice when they got pregnant. The tenure of female workers used to be shorter than that of men. That's reversed now. What that means for the parenting cycle remains to be seen.

But what are older moms like, and how are we changing the economy? First, it's all about spending as much time with the kids as we can, even though we're in the prime time of our careers. That means we negotiate for alternative benefits like flextime and work-from-home days instead of simply demanding more money to pay a nanny or enroll the kids in after-school programs to keep them busy until we get home. Remember Marissa Mayer, who had a nursery built into her office at Yahoo? She was thirty-seven when she had that baby.

And those kids get a lot of attention and money invested in them. If you thought previous generations were pampered, wait till you see the millennial moms' kids. They get all the resources of parents who are older and more economically secure. After all, mom gave up a lot to get to the point where she could get these kids. In many cases, the family has also spent a fortune simply to make the pregnancy happen in the first place. Fertility treatments tend to start at thirty-five, so the window is fairly short. The process can be expensive, which explains why in vitro fertilization stocks like Cooper Companies have been on an upward trajectory in recent years.

But as the biological clock ticks, millennial moms want to make sure they get the baby of their dreams rather than trust the details to nature.

They might get only one shot, so while they're in the clinic, they may pay extra to select the sex or screen for other traits. And there are a lot of multiple births. These kids will be the baby boom of the future.

Getting Disruption on Your Side

Companies like Chobani are a great place to start as we look for investment themes that the Echo Boom will feed. While this yogurt maker isn't public yet, the potential is gleaming just over the market horizon. It's the kind of IPO to anticipate. When Hamdi Ulukaya, a native of Turkey, moved to the United States in 2005, he discovered that yogurt was not as available or as delicious as it was in Turkey, so he bought a recently closed Kraft yogurt plant and launched Chobani, a brand that focused on quality and natural ingredients.

The company has several beliefs that appeal to the health-conscious millennial population. It uses only natural sweeteners, local milk, and non-GMO ingredients. The company even tends to the welfare of the cows in its dairy.

Millennials are interested not only in the product but also in what the company is doing for the greater good. Chobani is one of the companies that are working hard to make a difference. In fact, it gives 10 percent of its profits to charity through its Chobani Foundation. The company is heavily invested in its upstate New York and Idaho communities. It even built a state-of-the-art youth baseball stadium and community center in New Berlin, New York. In fact, Ulukaya recently announced that he would give all of his two thousand employees awards that could be worth up to 10 percent of the company's future value if it were to go public or be sold.

In February 2016, Chobani rejected an offer from PepsiCo. It was reported that Chobani wanted to sell only a minority stake, but PepsiCo wanted a majority. In 2013, the company had revenues of $1.2 billion and a 36.7 percent share of the Greek yogurt market, according to Nielsen data. Experts suspect this food niche will grow 5 percent each year, reaching four billion dollars in 2019. We expect Chobani to keep growing as millennials pursue healthier lives.

That means active lives. One brand that has made its mark on the athletic leisure wear industry is Lululemon, founded in 1998 in Canada to produce technical athletic apparel for women and men. The original store in Vancouver was a design studio during the day and a yoga studio at night. Since then, the company has seen incredible growth and has attracted a huge following.

Lululemon appeals to the consumer who wants to work out and look good while sweating, but what interests us is the way management has pursued new ideas in clothes. LULU's radio frequency identification system allows its employees to track products accurately as they move from warehouses to the stores, increasing its inventory accuracy to 98 percent.

One of the main reasons millennials love LULU is that it rewards customers and the community. Every week, all of its stores put their products aside and become yoga studios. An instructor leads a complimentary class for anyone who cares to attend. Nuances like this make millennials feel valued and happy that the company is not interested solely in the bottom line.

Meanwhile, tomorrow's consumers are growing up on Planet Starbucks. Echo Boomers love the convenience and the consistency. No matter which location you go to; from New York to California, an iced caramel macchiato is going to taste the same. Mobile order and delivery have eliminated lines and provide beverages on demand. The credit card never even has to come out. You pay by tapping your phone, and then you're out the door again.

Once that happens, the company's rewards program opens the door to a universe of in-app purchases and, in theory, advertising-supported partnerships. You probably recognize the trend by now: Echo Boomers love the way the company gives back to society. Around the world, the chain is working with young mothers, providing emergency diaper kits and training baristas to warm milk bottles. The customers love it.

While the specifics vary from company to company, this blurred edge between corporate realities, consumer choices, and matters of conscience is the future. The children of tomorrow identify with brands according to the aspirational worlds dreamed up in marketing meetings and made real through store design, supply-chain decisions, hiring choices, and all the other fine details. You're not just buying coffee here. You're buying a four-dollar ticket to a world that may or may not exist.

Unintended Consequences

Every trend has its shadow, providing challenges alongside the investment opportunities. Behind all the upbeat chatter, the millennial generation truly did come of age in the least forgiving economic environment since the 1940s, if not the Great Depression itself. If they'd grown up in more settled economic circumstances, they'd already be well on their way to a settled middle age, with children of their own moving up in school, well-established career paths complete with retirement accounts, suburban spread, and so on.

Instead, today's thirty-somethings got caught in at least one deep recession at a statistically painful moment in their economic lifecycle. Finding your first job out of school is a lot harder when all the adults are getting laid off, as we saw in 2000–2001 and again in 2008–2009. With paid positions of any description in tight supply, a lot of newly-minted workers simply aren't going to find work in their chosen field that pays the bills.

As a result, household formation has been delayed and sometimes tentative—a lot of millennials have already become homeowners, but millions more are still working toward that goal. They waited to have kids until they found the right place to raise them. The oldest of them are paying off their student debt in time to send their oldest kids to college. The youngest are those kids, getting their first jobs and taking the first steps toward starting their own households.

The Bottom Line for Early Adopters

Millennials are teaching their children to pursue "experiences" above possessions, spending their time and money on exquisitely curated social media journals instead of cleaning up the house. The travel industry has adjusted to reach the Echo Boom, and since many millennials waited until later in life to get married and have kids, they're now focused on kid-friendly hospitality as well as kid-free alternatives.

That said, this generation is feeling good, and when they have young children, spending doubles. As the millennials begin to grow older and move into jobs in which their salaries will continue to rise, we will see increased demand for long trips to exotic places where they can impress friends with vacation pictures, posted online of course.

Start with them. They're going to need apartments. Odds are good they'll have to share rentals in the hot housing markets where they love to live—Seattle, Memphis, Austin, Boston—but we're going to see new construction pick up once developers acknowledge that supply has lagged behind demand for too long. As today's renters advance in their careers and hustle up better opportunities, they'll graduate to bigger and better residential arrangements, if that's what they want.

And don't forget, these "kids" are only the trailing end of the millennial boom. Their older brothers and sisters may have graduated between the dot-com and housing crashes, but that was a long time ago, and they've found a way to build careers and lives for themselves. They're not waiting for the old economy to recover its pre-2008 momentum. They're living in the new economy, and each Baby Boomer who retires shifts the balance a little further in their favor.

CHAPTER TWO

Computing Power Out of Pocket: The Internet of Things

Think about the commonplace devices that were still science fiction a generation ago. Start with the personal fitness tracker, a Fitbit or Apple Watch. It's a very simple design: a small microcontroller, often built into a watch, that monitors your heart rate and one or more sensors that register when you take a step.

On its own, your watch can now tell you how many steps you've taken in a day or how your heart rate has varied over time. You have a portable EKG on your wrist. That's somewhat useful but at best minimally interesting—in the grand scheme of things, a novelty.

But you can store the collected data somewhere and correlate them with data pulled in from other devices via wireless frequencies. Say the portable EKG can access the mobile phone you carry everywhere with you. That phone is always collecting basic location information and a reliable timestamp, even if you haven't enabled GPS tracking. (It needs to know which tower it's talking to.) The day is coming soon when you'll be able to authorize the EKG to call 911 if it detects unusual cardiac stress. It will use your phone to make the call. The paramedics will know exactly where you are and what condition you'll be in when they arrive.

That's the Internet of Things: devices communicating with each other without your mediation, theoretically on your behalf.

Little Sensors Everywhere

Most people who've spent any time around Silicon Valley have at least heard of Moore's Law, the rule of innovation that says that the amount of computing power you can cram into the same area at the same price point doubles, more or less, every eighteen months.

Every investor knows how dramatic truly exponential growth can be even in a short period. (I wouldn't mind following a law that says I'd double my money every year and a half!) Double becomes quadruple which becomes octuple, and so on. Computing power has been expanding at that rate since 1950. As a result, applications that would once have required massive amounts of room and money are now available to every child with a touchscreen device or music player.

And you can choose in which direction you want to follow progress. If you maximize for scale, the bulky processors that ran the first Intel computers or helped control air force fighters back in the early 1970s are now measured in nanometers, hundreds of times smaller than a human cell. Or if you maximize for cost, that same 1970s chip that cost one thousand dollars is now practically free to manufacture.

Either way, we're only a few breakthroughs away from being able to cover the world with hundreds of billions of tiny computers, each powerful enough to perform basic mechanical tasks and make simple observations about its environment. They don't need to be any smarter than that as long as they can interact with a more powerful device somewhere within their network range. That's where the "Internet" in the Internet of Things comes into play.

And when you get enough crude processors working in parallel and exchanging data, they don't even need a lot of oversight. Cheap, low-power, ubiquitous computing opens up possibilities unlike anything that has come before. Even today, all sorts of "Things" in your immediate vicinity, many nominally under your control, have started merrily chattering away with each other.

The Opposite of "Killer Apps"

The challenge for programmers is figuring out how to make these multitudinous and microscopic devices useful and even essential parts of our everyday lives. The solution is convenience. As the world gets more complicated, we crave a way to delegate routine tasks to free up more time and brainpower for what truly matters to us. But if each of our devices needs to become a better servant, to quote the Robert Altman movie, it needs to learn how to "anticipate" our needs even before we ourselves know what we want.

That means a lot of monitoring of our behavior to detect patterns. Think about the way the autocorrect function on your phone learned to accept words you use and now suggests the ones you use most. A smart device needs to be able to "read" your contextual cues well enough to avoid sending a false signal or jumping to wrong conclusions that take your time and attention to correct.

Go back to that fitness monitor watching your heart minute to minute. A typical day might begin with a brief low-activity period followed by a thirty-minute high-heart-rate period that generally stays within a mile or so of the place you slept but seems to plot a fairly random course day by day. Then your phone notes that you've shifted to your second normal weekday location, where activity remains low until noon, when another twenty to thirty minutes of mildly elevated heart rate are followed by another long sedentary period and then a rapid move back to the initial location.

What have you been doing during all this? The devices have learned where you live, that you like to go for a half-hour run before work, where you work, how sedentary your job is, and that you like to go for a walk after lunch to get your blood moving again.

That's just two sensors. When you add a dozen or so more, a much sharper picture of your life emerges. Let's say you turn on finer-grained location services because you drive yourself to work and want Waze or a similar traffic-routing app to tell you which roads to avoid. Your credit and debit card companies know when and where you make purchases. Your phone probably has some kind of voice search so Siri or Alexa knows what you asked about and when. And your phone also has a microphone, which you gave some application permission to access whenever it wants.

With that sort of data, the things around you can correlate where you're spending your money with where your heart rate goes up. They learn that if you go to the Apple Store in the evening, you get excited by looking at the displays, but grocery shopping fails to grab you in the same way. Great! They won't call in a cardiac event at the Apple Store, but if you get excited at the supermarket, the devices of the future will either ask you to confirm that you're okay or reach out directly to alert your physician's device.

When You're the Product

Of course not all of the apps are on your side. There's a digital devil on your shoulder too. If you use Waze, you know that it shows you ads for nearby services when you're stopped at lights. Right now it's only vaguely annoying, but imagine that you've generated enough sensor data for the ad selection algorithm to know your habits better than you do.

One day in the future, your sensors have recognized that even though it was a relatively low-activity day, your heart rate is high. You're probably stressed. When you're in this state, you occasionally visit a particular bar on the way home from work, where your credit card records show you usually order a whiskey sour followed by a beer.

This time around, on the drive home, your phone chimes and tells you that it has "taken the liberty" of ordering a Bulleit Bourbon sour at Charlie's, which will be ready at half-price when you arrive in fifteen minutes. The discount also applies to the Anchor Steam you may want next, if you choose to order it.

The phone is thoughtful, even a little apologetic: "If I have misunderstood and you just want to go home, stay on your route home rather than diverting to Charlie's, and I will cancel the order." What do you do?

We aren't even talking about a malicious hack that interrupts your devices and throws their helpful suggestions off balance. These temptations are still a relatively "innocent" application of modern marketing techniques, as though the bar had paid to have a billboard erected along your route. The devices only want to make you happy. The advertisers that communicate with them don't necessarily want you to be healthy. They simply want to take your money.

Meanwhile, other people will use these same technologies to query local devices for patterns lurking within your behavior. Your physician will one day get better information about what you're eating from the kitchen sink and refrigerator than from talking to you. (And if you cheat too much on your approved heart-safe diet, the insurance company will probably weigh in.)

If you are in the habit of cheating your way through job interviews, you may want to learn some meditation techniques so your skin flush, pupil dilation, and heart rate don't betray you to the hiring manager's array of sensors. Know that when you meet someone, he may already know a lot about you. (This is, of course, already true. Body language and other subliminal cues already transmit huge amounts of information. It's just that the apps and sensors provide a data trail to support what the interviewer would once have called intuition.)

And all this information keeps circulating across the network, below the level where human beings will ever see it without making a huge effort. Remember, we don't interact with the Internet of Things apart from specially designed interfaces like touch screens, voice controls, and old-fashioned keyboards. This is a world where billions of computer processors, invisible to human eyes, share data with each other.

Consider the now-familiar data breach. As I write this, Capital One has just announced that more than 100 million credit card accounts have been exposed. How many times over the past year have you been

informed that the database of some company you did business with has
been hacked and your vital statistics are now on the Dark Web? How
many times have you actually been fraudulently charged and ended up
having to pay anything?

Overseas mobsters don't care about you. Your credit card is one line
out of ten million in a database. It's statistically unlikely to be the one
chosen for a fraudulent purpose, and if it is, that purchase will be different enough from your usual purchasing patterns that the card company's
own pattern-matching apps will flag the transaction. You're more likely
to run into trouble if your physical card is lost, stolen, or simply misap-
propriated by someone close to you. (This vulnerability of the physical
card is driving Apple's efforts to make it irrelevant by shifting transactions to the phone itself, but that's another story.)

More generally, privacy is no longer absolute… if it ever was. There's
always at least one eye in the sky observing all our acts down here on earth.
The only real solution in a world of surveillance is to stop doing things
that would embarrass you or get over the shame. Amazon knows where
we live and what we buy, but so did the neighborhood storekeeper a generation ago. Google knows where you drive, and one day smart cars will
too, but that's not much different from a police cruiser tailing someone
while it looks for a suspect driving a similar make and model vehicle.

You might also worry about a corrupt governmental system using
its dossier against you. Whenever I mention this, a friend of mine always
points out what a theologian who grew up in totalitarian East Germany
once told her: "You worry too much. If the cops want you, they're as lazy
as everyone else. They're not going to bother to find something you did
wrong, they're just going to make something up."

The Smart Home

The Internet of Things doesn't stop when you come home, either.
You can turn off your smart appliances like Alexa or the Google Home,
but if convenience is the point, it's hard to beat a little box you can simply

instruct to turn the lights off when you leave the room or to have a hot meal waiting for you when you return.

Alexa can already order household products on your behalf as fast as you manage to consume them. You'll never run out. Smart refrigerators on the horizon will make sure you never run out of food. Authorize Alexa to order from Whole Foods and have dinner delivered, or if it queries your phone and sees that you're already near the supermarket, the fridge can even send you a text message letting you know what you need to buy. Early applications aren't quite so ambitious (they'll text you if you leave the door open), but it's all just a way to work out the interface. They'll talk if you leave the door open.

Smart sinks will dispense exactly as much water as you want at the temperature you specify, eliminating both waste and measuring cups. Smart switches know which rooms are empty and which need the lights left on. Vacuum cleaners work on their own throughout, always out of sight. These are relatively "dumb" devices, with at best the processing power of a first-generation ATM kiosk or modern candy vending machine.

Some will be smarter than others. Alexa or a similar data hub (call it a "concierge") will listen for what you need, delegate tasks via wireless signal, and then anticipate how to do it more efficiently next time. Home automation can already reduce overall household energy demand by 40 percent today.

You can always override if you want a room hotter or colder, brighter or darker, although the hub may query you and your medical sensors to make sure you aren't coming down with a virus. In that scenario, the ambulance is always just an automated call away, and it might even arrive on its own if the sensors recognize patterns that line up with distress and call in first.

And the odds are good that most of it will play music and video, albeit on small speakers and screens. The stereo is everywhere. The television may be nothing more than a large-scale screen camouflaged as wall art when it's not in streaming mode.

Getting Disruption on Your Side

Figuring out how to make money off ubiquitous computing is more difficult than simply leaning back and enjoying the ease it brings to your daily life. There are two sides to this equation: data creators and data aggregators.

The aggregator side is easiest. This is the FAAMG group of gigantic Silicon Valley companies: Facebook, Amazon, Apple, Microsoft, and Google. Unfortunately, they are already among the biggest enterprises on the planet, so while they make good long-term investments, you're not going to get eye-popping returns from any of them in the near term. As I say, they're great companies, but their best days as stocks are past. We're here to participate in the future.

That said, some of these giants are more vulnerable than others. Apple makes a lot of noise over the privacy of your data, and its business model, unlike the rest, is selling you electronics, as opposed to selling your data. But with so much vital information routed through Apple devices, this trillion-dollar company is never more than one major data breach and three successive disappointing products from total collapse. And now there's no Steve Jobs to step back in and save it.

Facebook and Google are barely better. Amazon probably has the best record on user privacy on the consumer side—and remember, the real function of Alexa and other Amazon devices is to collect information on your habits to sell you more merchandise. Jeff Bezos doesn't want that data getting out, especially if would-be rivals could get their hands on it.

Overseas, China generates vast amounts of data across a population four times as large as the United States, but the stocks are opaque. Alibaba or Tencent might be good bets, but the lack of transparency around these stocks makes investment in Chinese data companies unavoidably risky. Nevertheless, the size and technological sophistication of the Chinese market—and the lack of cultural expectation of privacy—reminds us that there's an enormous amount of data being collected and analyzed in non-U.S. populations as well.

Don't forget that there are also a billion people in India. Onerous EU data protection laws make the EU a less attractive area for investment in the data-aggregation side of ubiquitous computing than elsewhere.

There are also industries that have borne a heavy burden of data-rights regulation which, if relaxed, there open new opportunities. Health-care is a good example. While HIPAA privacy rules are strict today, encryption could let hospitals, insurance carriers, and doctors share patient vital signs as "openly" as banks move balance information around today. And if not, all they need to do is sign the release and opt into their program.

Keep an eye on the large healthcare providers like Cigna and also on smaller data analytics firms within the same field. Look for new approaches to the "electronic medical record," and pay especially close attention to shifts in personal genetic data regulation. Yes, this seems largely like settled law at this point, but statutes can change.

Where you are more likely to make a ground-floor investment that explodes is in companies that generate data through new devices and apps that give everyday people an incentive to authorize the sensors to start recording. Remember, almost all startups fail, and consumer electronics is a harsh business. If you bought into Fitbit or GoPro five years ago, you're sitting on losses of 90 to 95 percent.

Finally, consider where all the bandwidth to keep all these devices talking will come from, not to mention the operating systems that structure their programs, keep the data flowing, and lock out opportunistic intruders. The rollout of 5G networking isn't about better signal for us humans. In most areas wireless telephony outpaced old-school wired-call quality long ago. More spectrum is required to support what's likely to be 75 billion separate connections a mere five years from now. Extrapolate the trend to 2050 and there could be two trillion devices chirping silently at each other, each needing its separate signal to avoid confusion.

That's a lot of signal. Odds are good that a lot of it will come from new forms of satellite connectivity. Conventional terrestrial networks will have to handle the rest of the load, with contracts going to people who develop faster, cheaper, and more efficient processing techniques. After all, Moore's Law hasn't hit its limit yet. Devices are getting smaller, cheaper, and more numerous. Networks need to make room or get out of the way.

Unintended Consequences

The losers in this scenario are pretty obvious. If you're a retailer who isn't plugged into the way devices of the future "nudge" consumer decisions, you won't even show up on the map. That's not an extinction-level choice, but it makes it hard to stay relevant as digital natives rise in economic prominence and ignore anything they can't see on their phones.

But life will go on as always in regions of the world where broadband networks remain underbuilt or even nonexistent, at least for a few years or decades longer. As Moore's Law marches on, the cost of the smartphone device tends towards zero, and the cost of the chips that power the towers and satellites drops as well.

One day soon, if you live in an area too remote to connect your appliances to each other and to the Big Data platforms behind them all, it will be by choice. Turn it off, opt out, drop out. You can use what will by 2050 be considered old-fashioned credit cards (or even cash) and debate trivia with human beings and textbooks instead of the voice-activated research system that inhabits your personal data ecosystem. The advertisements won't follow you wherever you go.

We're looking for a resurgence of small and local or at most regional retail behind the Internet of Things. Granted, the global brands will get bigger and reach deeper into consumer life as the cities get denser. Some may even subsidize even cheaper devices and the bandwidth to support them. That's their business, literally. Shareholders will participate in the profits either way.

The Bottom Line for Early Adopters

Get over yourself. Your personal data are not especially interesting unless you have something extremely special to hide, and even then most of the people with access to that information have seen it all before. If you're actually worried about your own privacy and the security of your own personal information, you've already lost.

Everything about you is already known to the Chinese and Russian mafias and governments (to the degree those are separable entities), to federal agencies, to Google, to Amazon, to your insurance carrier, and even your phone. Relax. You live in public. The house is always listening. If you want to be alone, turn it off.

But within the Internet of Things, you receive the kind of personalized service, with exquisite attention paid to your personal preferences, that used to be reserved for the rich and powerful. Everything around you focuses on you, the bright center of a world of robotic servants chattering behind the scenes about how to anticipate your every desire.

Existing predictive models can already guess your cravings with such accuracy that Google's advertising algorithm really does know you better than you know yourself. The true Internet of Things will make sure your refrigerator is always stocked with the right mix of healthy foods you enjoy, that the ambient music always suits your mood, and that your biometric sensors continually read something between enthusiasm and delight.

So lean into the future. Let your car recommend where to gas up as long as you buy twenty-five dollars' worth of groceries at the store that's partnered with the gas station (and shares a parking lot). Your refrigerator called: You need a gallon of milk, some onions, and a new pack of dish towels anyway. Your heart monitor knows it's been a stressful week, but you've made your exercise and weight targets. Why not indulge with the three-packs-for-ten-dollars Oreo special? Just don't accept that free drink at Charlie's.

CHAPTER THREE

THE AUTONOMOUS CAR: SAFE AT MAXIMUM SPEED

Learning to drive wasn't easy, but it's practically a universal experience, so I was both perplexed and intrigued when my daughter said she didn't want to bother. She's part of the reason that self-driving cars are being tested on today's roads for imminent mass-market deployment. And when they hit the road, our basic assumptions are going to change quickly.

It may take a while before we get the flying cars that the Jetsons enjoyed, but when our cars drive themselves, we'll have a lot more time to relax, read, and communicate with our families. That future is rapidly approaching. Are you still in the slow lane fighting to get to the exit ramp, or would you rather hit the cruise control and coast?

How Smart Cars See

For decades, auto manufacturers experimented with self-driving vehicles that needed their own environment defined by magnetic strips or other route markers. Nothing got in their way because nothing else was allowed on the track. The self-driving cars of today and tomorrow need to be self-governing to travel the same roads as the rest of us, with full control of their movements. They plot their own routes with GPS and use sensors and advanced AI to negotiate traffic.

This is about more than being able to scroll through Facebook while you're driving to work. It's practically reinventing the wheel. The sensor technology alone is revolutionary. LIDAR (light detection and ranging) is one of the most promising ways to build up a three-dimensional picture of each car's surroundings, accurate within a millimeter at a hundred-foot range. These vehicles see a lot more than debris on the road or a child jumping off the sidewalk in front of them. They know the shape of the buttons on your jacket from across the street.

Waymo, the company that originated as Google's self-driving taxi project, has developed LIDAR systems so effective that they plan to offset their own development costs by selling sensor equipment to other industries, such as security, warehousing, and agriculture. This is now one of the companies most likely to bring sight to the entire automated world, and those eyes will always be open across a 360-degree spherical range.

These incredible eyes need a reliable brain to interpret the massive flood of sensory data and turn it into decisions. Machines start at a disadvantage here, since driving a car requires human skills and instincts that evolution has been refining for millions of years. But as we'll see in Chapter Four, machine-learning systems in the age of the Internet have a big advantage over human beings: they learn *collectively*, whereas we learn *individually*. All smart cars are as smart as the smartest smart car.

Driving in icy conditions is a difficult skill, and if I want to acquire it, I have to practice and learn it myself. Knowing someone who lives in northern Canada won't help me unless I go up there and get her to give me some lessons. Self-driving cars can benefit from software updates based on the experiences of the entire fleet. Every accident, every incident, every mistake, and every nuance gets recorded.

That's why fleet miles on the road are the best gauge of an autonomous vehicle platform's expertise. The average American drives less than fourteen thousand miles a year, or around 700,000 miles across a fifty-year span. Waymo cars collectively drove 1.2 million miles in 2018 alone, and the passenger had to take the wheel barely a hundred times the whole distance. That intervention rate is dropping 50 percent every twelve months. Within the next decade, the most advanced fleets will have seen it all and know how to react in any situation.

The City Where Robot Taxis Never Need To Park

In congested urban centers, it's not hard to imagine a future where everyone who owns his own vehicle needs to park remotely and then travel by automated taxi within city limits. The sidewalks will belong to people, and the streets will belong to robots, which even today face their greatest challenges when a bad human driver gets in their way.

When they aren't being repaired or refueled, they never need to stop moving. I've seen statistics that show 30 percent of all traffic moving through San Francisco today is looking for a parking space. That number may be as high as 80 percent in Paris. If nobody needs to park, the space (maybe as much as 30 percent of a typical city's urban footprint) can be reclaimed for housing or commercial applications. According to McKinsey, we're looking at 61 billion square feet of real estate in the U.S. alone, worth at least nine trillion dollars.

And since self-driving cars can communicate with each other over wireless networks, they need to signal turns only as a courtesy to us. Intersection etiquette is not only observed but regulated to route every vehicle efficiently, clearing the way for emergency vehicles while directing flow around bottlenecks. (In some scenarios, a stubborn human-operated vehicle becomes the bottleneck that the fleet needs to negotiate.)

From what I've seen in New York, gridlock can eventually hit a point where some cities will encourage this kind of universal adoption and close the streets to human drivers, at least on week days, at rush hour, or on some other flexible basis. It's not like driving in town is fun for most people anyway, and parking is a nightmare.

We'll also get a lot more done. People in the world's most congested cities would collectively recover 250 million hours of commuting time for getting ahead on the day's work, catching up on lost sleep, or simply goofing off with their onboard screens. Service providers could ride along to style our hair, consult with us on our taxes, prepare a meal, or conduct a medical test, getting out at the next stop to rendezvous with their next client. For some, the car itself could become a traveling conference room, although at that point the real question is why you'd bother going to the office at all.

Who Owns the Car?

The ability to take a car journey without driving will change our entire perception of road transport. With high-bandwidth mobile internet, a lengthy commute can become a productive part of the working day, cutting the hours you need to spend at the office because you can work on the way. Longer commutes will therefore become more tolerable, reviving property prices in rural areas and driving a new wave of development. For long journeys with the family or friends, sleeper vehicles will allow you to travel in comfort while offering a cheaper alternative to domestic flights. Many of the advantages of rail travel will be replicated on the road, but with increased privacy, flexibility, and comfort.

Of course the automobile has been a symbol of personal freedom since its invention. Ownership of a car brought the world to you, letting you set off for an impulse trip on a Saturday morning without having to check train timetables. The word "automobile" itself suggested autonomy, and the car naturally became a crucial component of the human psyche, at least here in New Jersey.

For decades the car has defined the socioeconomic status of its owner. It is often the most expensive thing anyone will ever buy besides a house, an extended course of medical treatment, or a college education. CEOs and celebrities have garages full of them, and until recently teenagers were always eager to get ahold of the keys. We don't know yet how the autonomous vehicle revolution will affect the cult of the car. Perhaps the two markets will find an equilibrium, with privately-owned vehicles driven for leisure and pleasure while robo-taxis handle the commute and robo-trucks haul goods through the night.

Alternatively, we could see a near-wholesale adoption of the autonomous vehicle, driven perhaps by safety and environmental concerns or perhaps by simple economics. Fully autonomous cars, built to last but complicated to maintain, will be extremely efficient and expensive by today's standards. Private ownership of the vehicle may remain symbolic while the pragmatic cost of ownership pushes the rest of us to hail the local taxi.

Accelerating to Racing Gear

The transition to an autonomous world won't happen overnight. It will take place in stages, self-driving vehicles being limited to closely delineated spaces and certain times of day, much as those first automated cars ran on their own programmed tracks like trains.

The National Highway Traffic Safety Administration has defined five levels of vehicle automation, from zero to full control. Don't invest assuming that fully-automatic Level 5 vehicles will be in every driveway within a few years. Many businesses are involved in the industry; many of them have their own proprietary technology. It will take some time to work out all the bugs. Once someone discovers a dramatically better way to do something, everyone will start doing it.

What we are likely to see early on for personal autonomous vehicles is the adoption of the technology by affluent non-drivers, and this could begin by the 2020s or the 2030s. These early adopters would pave the way for later use of the technology. During that time, systems would come online for reducing parking problems and traffic congestion, along with the added benefits of better safety features, energy savings, reduced pollution, and better mobility for low-income and older persons.

These benefits will be more widespread as autonomous vehicles and the infrastructure supporting them become less expensive and more common, probably in the 2040s and into the 2050s. But self-driving taxis, vans, and other autonomous short-distance services will become commonplace in urban areas starting in the 2020s and 2030s. While the ride services will be cheaper than the human-driven taxis of today, the quality of service will be lower: no one to help with luggage, open doors, or clean rubbish out of the passenger area.

Companies like May Mobility are already looking at low-speed, high-density urban environments as the testing ground for shared-ride vehicles. Such areas, where large numbers of people live and work, are ideal subjects for automated-vehicle research. The number of high-speed individual vehicles could be reduced because automation and coordination will greatly increase the mobility and efficiency of the traffic flow. In New York at rush hour, traffic moves so slowly that it doesn't take a lot of brainpower at all to keep up with the flow. Accidents will be rare, and speeds will be low enough that few if any will amount to more than a nudge.

We'll gradually look at transportation differently. There may be some personal autonomous vehicles at first, those that someone would lease or own for himself. Shared autonomous vehicles would be like taxis, Uber, or Lyft ridesharing. Shared autonomous ride vehicles would replace trams or buses, taking passengers to pre-determined stops near their ultimate destinations, reducing the need for "park and ride" areas.

Getting Disruption on Your Side

The market for passenger transport will grow steadily over the next decade and then experience a rapid boom when the technology reaches maturity and legislatures have had time to adapt to the realities of the driverless economy. A study commissioned by Intel in 2017 and prepared by Strategy Analytics describes the "Passenger Economy" as a mosaic of ride-hailing and other mobility-as-a-service solutions, powered by autonomous vehicle technology. Demand for these services may reach a staggering $7 trillion by 2050.

The technological journey of Google's self-driving car project, Waymo, has been impressive. In the beginning, it needed to shell out seventy-five thousand dollars for each LIDAR sensor package, but after redeveloping this critical system in-house, it has lowered its cost by a reported 90 percent. Waymo is working in partnership with a number of companies including Intel (which in turn bought another robot vision company, Mobileye), but the most exciting collaboration at the moment was started in 2017 with the ride-hailing service Lyft.

All the major auto manufacturers are involved in various projects and partnerships to deliver self-driving technology, and there are far too many attempts and agendas to list here. But it's also worth thinking about companies that might get rich supplying technology to whoever manufactures the self-driving cars of the future. As an example, consider chipmaker NVIDIA, which has announced a plan to manufacture AI-specialized processing units tailored for autonomous vehicles.

We can't talk about self-driving vehicles without mentioning Tesla, founded and led by their premier evangelist, Elon Musk. Tesla's Autopilot feature, which still requires an attentive human being at the wheel, is the most widely used semi-autonomous driving system in the world. Musk is confident of offering a "fully self-driving" upgrade to Autopilot this year, a system he asserts will allow the driver to fall asleep safely at the wheel.

Getting a slice of the self-driving pie looks like a great idea, but it's a difficult bet. Every auto manufacturer and less traditional companies like Waymo, and maybe even Apple itself, are vying to develop the technology and corner the driverless market. How can an investor tell which is going to succeed? Do you trust in Tesla, which is probably overvalued for its current business (visionary company, difficult stock), in the hope that whatever Elon Musk does next will lead to a sustainable enterprise? Or do you stick with a more experienced auto manufacturer like Audi or General Motors?

An alternative is to take my preferred "picks and shovels" approach. Can we identify what technologies are going to be the price of entry to the autonomous vehicle market? LIDAR seems a risky bet since many companies, including Waymo, are designing their own system, and Tesla is not using the technology at all.

Investing in next-generation battery technology might be safer. The driverless world is an electric dream, and today's lithium-ion batteries aren't up to the job. Sila Nanotechnologies is working on the next step with extensive investment from Daimler. And while self-driving vehicles will do a lot of information-processing onboard, reliable and high-bandwidth internet connections will be essential. The 5G network infrastructure will eventually allow cities to operate networks of sensors to support self-driving vehicles. Verizon doesn't make self-driving cars, but if you believe in the technology, it might not make a bad investment.

Don't rule out the ride-sharing networks here. They'll own the fleets and run a lot more efficiently when the drivers are out of the loop. Lyft and Waymo recently partnered to operate a fleet of several hundred Waymo One robo-taxis in Phoenix. This staging ground will provide important feedback from early adopters and test the advanced technology of Waymo's vehicles. At present, a human "safety driver" remains in the driver's seat in case he is needed, but the Waymo One vehicles are capable of driving fully autonomously, routinely completing their journeys without intervention by the safety driver.

Lyft users in Las Vegas have also been taking self-driving taxis (with safety drivers). Since May 2018, Las Vegas residents have been able to use the Lyft app to hail one of a fleet of thirty BMW 5-series sedans, extensively modified for autonomous driving. The Irish auto parts and mobility solutions company Aptiv supplies the self-driving technology. Lyft and Aptiv have logged more than fifty thousand journeys in Las Vegas.

Lyft's biggest competitor, Uber, is also looking forward to the driverless age. Unfortunately, the road there has been rocky. In 2018, a forty-nine-year-old woman in Tempe, Arizona, was struck and killed by one of Uber's experimental autonomous vehicles. The vehicle did not stop or slow down, and the safety driver did not intervene quickly enough to prevent the accident. Uber shut down its testing operations in Arizona and halted all testing for nine months, finally tiptoeing back into the field with a modified Volvo XC90. Uber and Volvo say the new version will be safer from day one, but the shadow of the fatal accident still looms over the project.

More and more people are becoming comfortable with the idea of Uber- and Lyft-style ride-sharing apps, where one can request a ride and find a willing driver to pick them up. Soon, the same kind of app will be able to request a vehicle on standby or to divert one already on the move to the passenger's location. That could be what it takes to get me to embrace one or both stocks.

Unintended Consequences

With all of this wonderful technology on the horizon, someone has to lose. Somewhere, someone is making the twenty-first-century equivalent of the buggy-whip. Taxi and truck drivers will be obsolete, and future generations will find the very idea of such jobs archaic, like the telephone exchange operators of the past. Fixed-route public transport like subways and traditional buses, which leave many areas underserved, will disappear in favor of the convenience and ubiquity of ride-hailing apps.

If transportation-as-a-service takes over the roads, private car owner-ship will dwindle. The demand for local mechanics, car dealers, car washes, and auto parts stores will vanish, no longer consumer-facing businesses but functions of the corporate infrastructure to support fleets of self-driving vehicles. Driving schools will cater to a niche market of traditionalists and racing drivers.

Self-driving cars will bring cities and other destinations closer together. The ability to go to sleep in a self-driving car and wake up for breakfast in a new city will make travel over a few hundred miles much more attractive and eliminate the need to stop in a motel along the way. As long as you get a long-range car with a bathroom, there will be no problem.

Never forget the effect on ancillary service providers. If the number of human-driven cars on the road drops by as much as 90 percent and all the other traffic is programmed to go with the flow, accident rates will drop precipitously, and so will auto insurance enrollments. Investment geniuses like Warren Buffett have placed big long-term bets on the assumption that car insurance will always be a cash machine. Maybe not.

On the other hand, the insurance companies may welcome the widespread use of autonomous vehicles. Costs could drop because of a decrease in automobile crashes. The risk could change from the mistakes of drivers to the mistakes of manufacturers or the contractors responsible for the infrastructure. Such cases could delay implementation of the technology until the novel legal questions are settled.

Some of the costs will follow from the technology itself. If vehicle miles traveled increase, the infrastructure must be in place to support it, otherwise there will be congested streets and increased fuel costs. Policy makers need to balance the up-front costs of the necessary infrastructure with the projected savings when pitching the ideas to the public.

Parking lots and garages could suffer a loss of revenue if autonomous vehicles constantly drive their routes without the need to park. While the facilities themselves could be adapted for other uses, many cities rely on the revenue from parking meters, parking lots, and parking tickets. Investors may need to reevaluate their holdings in urban mass transit and bus companies if works projects are delayed or cancelled because autonomous vehicles now fill those roles.

Police departments, particularly in rural areas, might see their revenues from speeding tickets dry up. Autonomous vehicles such as those networked together in a train or platoon would be capable of speeds above the current speed limits, and those limits would need to be raised accordingly. Once the speed limits were reset, the vehicles wouldn't exceed them—speed governors would be part of the programming.

"Do-it-yourselfers" could have a difficult time in the era of the self-driving vehicle. Even today, cars have become so computerized and complex that repair jobs that could have been done easily in the past are now outside the reach of the amateur mechanic. In the automated future, there may be regulations concerning what maintenance can be performed by the owner or lessee. Most of the work, especially concerning the automated driving systems, will need to be performed by a licensed professional. There may even be tags and seals threatening voided warranties or revoked driving privileges.

One area that is not frequently mentioned in this space is the "car crash industry"—medical staff, lawyers, insurance companies, repair shops—that would be disrupted by a drop in motor vehicle accident rates. All of these fields would of course still exist, but they could see their business drop considerably.

The Bottom Line for Early Adopters

The futurists, Elon Musk included, have made grand promises for the speed with which autonomous vehicles will reach the market and from there conquer the world. They haven't done it yet. We still love our cars here in New Jersey, even if we hate the traffic.

Regardless of which companies make it big and how long they take to get off the ground, there's no stopping the wave of change that driverless technology will let loose. It stands to change how we commute and how we think of vehicle ownership. Freed from the driver's seat, we'll have more time for leisure or productive work, and new markets will arise to entertain and pamper us while we're on the move. Our roads will be less congested, our cities less crammed with ugly parking lots. The road ahead is cleaner, safer, and more exciting than ever before.

As luxury vehicles owned by communities or the elite, the cars of 2050 will be either flamboyant or practically unnoticed. Cost-conscious designs may look like moving mailboxes or fireplugs. Move up the price point scale, and you'll see things that leave the golden age of private railcars or corporate jets in the dust. The most lavish may even come with a human driver as the ultimate status symbol.

CHAPTER FOUR

"Beyond Meat" and Beyond: The Future of Food

How do you throw a dinner party for 10 billion people? That will be the biggest question facing the food industry in 2050. The United Nations projects that the world's population will increase by 2–3 billion in the next thirty years. That's a lot more hungry mouths to feed, and the solution won't be planting more corn and beets, either.

Agriculture already uses 50 percent of the world's vegetated land, and we can't turn the rest over to crops without severe consequences for our fragile environment. The farmers of tomorrow will need to grow more food using fewer resources. Food processors will need to reduce waste by using every part of a crop or food animal. Our diets will have to change, too, from inefficient foods to healthier and more sustainable alternatives.

Fortunately, a lot of the groundwork has already been laid. Agricultural production has leapt forward over the last decade, with higher crop yields and more milk and meat drawn from fixed resources. While Americans certainly haven't given up their love of hamburgers, they're increasingly willing to make them out of something other than beef.

Keeping Food on the Global Table

In 2012, the United Nations Food and Agriculture Organization projected that the world's agricultural production needs to increase by 60 percent over the production of 2005 to meet the food needs of 2050. Farmers are already well on their way to meeting that target. The gross value of worldwide agricultural production increased by 30 percent between 2005 and 2015, halfway to the goal with decades still to go.

A food revolution is underway in farms and labs around the world. At the Cold Spring Harbor Laboratory in New York, geneticists are using CRISPR techniques to edit the genes of tomato plants. The plants now produce twice as many branches and, as a result, twice as many tomatoes. Other projects include improving the nutritional value of plants and their resistance to drought and pests.

Gene-edited canola with more oil in its seeds is already on the market. Experiments are being conducted on corn, mushrooms, bananas, and cacao trees to improve yields and resistance to pests. Scientists are also trying to reduce the gluten content of wheat, making the grain more edible to the estimated 20 million Americans who are gluten-sensitive.

CRISPR editing isn't the only new food technology in play. Technologies that seem to have nothing to do with agriculture are improving agricultural operations. Dairy barns in North America and Europe are using facial recognition technology to track the health and behavior of their cows. Dairy farmers use software and analytics from the Dublin-based company Cainthus to adjust feeding plans and tend to sick animals.

In Spain, the industrial manufacturing company Hiperbaric has been a pioneer in high-pressure processing (HPP) for food. A "cold" pasteurization technique, HPP protects food by sealing it in packaging then submitting it to eighty-seven thousand pounds per square inch of water pressure. That's the equivalent of putting the package sixty kilometers below the ocean surface. The technique reduces waste and kills most microorganisms without affecting the texture and nutritional value of the food.

As much as a third of the food that the world currently produces is wasted, and reducing that waste is the focus of several startups. Smart Cara in South Korea produces food waste processors that break down excess food into a powder that can be used as fertilizer. The market for waste processors has been spurred by compulsory waste-food recycling with fees by the biodegradable bag. South Korea now recycles 95 percent of its food waste.

The Dutch company Protix feeds food waste to fly larvae, which then become food for chickens. The British company Entomics Biosystems, also in the fly larvae game, has been testing its products on Scottish salmon. The farm salmon are currently fed with fishmeal made from Peruvian anchovies, so a local, insect-based approach offers a lot of potential as a sustainable replacement.

The Ocean Floor's the Limit

The growing field of aquaculture is also a hotbed of innovation. Traditional fishmeal made from recycled fish parts is unlikely to keep up with demand, leading to new sources such as the fly-based fishmeal being developed by Entomics. Algae feed also shows promise. Established companies like Cargill and startups like KnipBio are working to reduce the high cost of algae feed and make it an economical feed source.

Algae aren't just fish food, either. Algae grown in New Mexican farms are already being used in protein bars and food supplements and have the potential to become a dietary staple. Algae grow well in dry environments with brackish water and can produce vast amounts of food with just a little carbon dioxide and sunlight.

Sustainability is a major concern as aquaculture is scaled up. Norway-based Nordic Aquafarms plans to build a $500 million land-based salmon farm in Belfast, Maine. It will use some of the world's largest aquaculture tanks, each one three times the size of an Olympic-sized swimming pool and capable of producing thirty-three thousand tons of fish per year. The tanks will recirculate water through filtration systems, avoiding the pollution and disease that afflict traditional open-air fish farms.

Recirculating technology has existed for years but is only now efficient enough to be applied to large farms. There's still a lot of work to be done. In Virginia, the Blue Ridge Aquaculture tilapia farm recirculates 85 percent of its water but still transports thousands of gallons of water each day to sewage plants. Its CEO, Bill Martin, hopes to increase the farm's recirculation technology to 99 percent efficiency and to produce electricity by capturing methane from the fish waste.

Other fish farms are pushing forward the technology of offshore aquaculture. The open ocean rapidly dilutes the waste produced by large concentrations of fish, keeping the fish healthier and reducing the need for antibiotics. Farming the open ocean is more challenging than penning up fish in rivers or protected coves, but when mastered it will provide more scalability with fewer environmental problems.

Not all of the techniques needed to master fish farming are new. Scientists in Canada are adapting traditional Chinese approaches to aquaculture and looking for ways to make them work on a larger scale. The Chinese farmers of a thousand years ago relied on polyculture to build an interlocking ecosystem of resources. Duck and pig manure would fertilize algae, which would be eaten by carp. The carp would eat pests and fertilize rice before being eaten themselves. This ancient system is still in use on Chinese farms today. The modern Canadian version feeds fish, then grows kelp and places shellfish and sea cucumbers downstream of the fish to filter the water. The Canadian scientists' goal is to build a modular system that can be plugged into aquaculture operations around the world.

The Sustainable "Hamburger"

The American consumer is ready to start eating something different. 2018 was a record year for American meat consumption at 222 pounds of red meat and poultry per capita. That's four times the world's average.

About a quarter of that consumption was beef, which has been slowly declining in popularity since the 1970s.

Fifty pounds of beef per person per year is still a lot of beef, and it is one of the least efficient food products in the world. Beef production uses seven times as much land per pound as chicken and produces seven times the greenhouse gas. The ratio to plant-based production is an even starker twenty to one.

Lab-grown meat is unlikely to answer that concern. In fact, a 2019 study shows that meat in a lab might produce even more greenhouse gas. To reduce the impact on the environment, Americans and other citizens of industrialized nations will have to shift away from meat to more efficient food products.

Growing plants affects the environment too, of course. Industrialized agriculture has relied heavily on monocultures and chemical fertilizers and pesticides. Soil depletion, toxic runoff, and population collapses among bees and other beneficial species all pose barriers to increasing production.

The sustainable farming movement will continue to gain steam as agribusiness tries to balance production, profit, and environmental impact. The traditional practices of growing diverse crops using biological fertilizers and pesticides are being refined by scientists looking for the most efficient combinations of species and techniques. Improvements in soil health, tilling practices, and planting methods and a return to the use of heirloom seeds show potential for improving the health and yield of crops.

We can also look elsewhere on the food chain. Insect farming is less efficient than plant farming but comparable to poultry and fish farming. Insects are only a little better at converting feed to protein than chicken or carp, but they use less land and emit fewer greenhouse gases. Given the relatively small differences in efficiency between insects and poultry, though, most Americans probably won't be switching to a bug-based diet any time soon.

Vat-Grown Superfood

Let's return to the algae. Already hailed as superfoods for their high nutritional content and intense flavors, algae and seaweed are gaining a presence on restaurant plates and supermarket shelves. The British grocer Sainsbury's sells a sausage with an algae casing, and Whole Foods Market reported an 11.5 percent rise in 2018 sales for chlorella powder, a chlorophyll-rich algae in powdered form.

The cyanobacterium spirulina, blue-green algae, is seeing increased use as a food additive. When dried, it is almost two-thirds protein, with plenty of B minerals and iron. It's showing up in ice cream, egg substitutes, and protein powders. It can also be added to soups, smoothies, hummus, and pasta doughs.

Most seaweeds are also classified as algae, even fifty-foot-long strands of kelp. They have a long history in seafaring cultures as salad greens, soup bases, and edible wrappings around fish and rice. Seaweed's profile is also rising in mass food culture. Tesco became the first major British grocer to stock fresh sea spaghetti in 2015.

These changes in food production and preparation won't happen in isolation. Food is an important part of culture, and cultures shift as they embrace new diets.

We've already seen this in past decades as American food brands such as McDonalds, KFC, and Coca-Cola have spread across the world. Some countries, such as Japan, have embraced American food brands as symbols of progress and prosperity. Others, such as France, have resisted the ruination of their national cuisines, but that hasn't stopped their youth from devouring American burgers and fries. The adoption of American food habits has had dramatic effects on both bodies and public health. Japanese youth grow up to be a foot taller and many pounds heavier than their grandparents and great-grandparents. Despite efforts by the French government, heart disease and diabetes are rising as the French supersize le Big Mac.

That trend will be reversed over the next thirty years. Producing enough food for the world's population to eat well is already a high bar.

Producing enough food for everyone to eat like an American is unrealistic and unnecessary. The well-balanced diet of 2050 will be a mix of traditional and technological foods from across world cultures.

Ironically, it may be the big American food brands that spread this new approach to food. In 2017, McDonalds tested out its McVegan potato-and-peas burger for seven weeks in Tampere, Finland. The product was a hit there and in Sweden and is now a part of the company's international menu.

Getting Disruption on Your Side

Feeding the world in 2050 will require global capabilities in research, development, and distribution. Long cycles of crop management and modification also favor companies with the scale and financing to pursue projects for years or even decades.

The market is growing in so many areas that it's hard to be sure about where to put your money. In 2015, however, McKinsey identified two dozen hot spots for investors to focus on. Aquaculture, agricultural machinery, and storage infrastructure in emerging markets were three of the biggest opportunities they pointed out. (They were also bullish on protein in China, but only if that protein was pork.)

McKinsey's approach is a sound one. As investors, our bets should be on the companies that will benefit from the expansion of the global food supply. In the agricultural machinery category, this includes companies like EM3 AgriServices, a startup in India that helps farmers rent their equipment to each other, or New Holland, which is developing a tractor powered by methane.

On the storage infrastructure front, China's cold chain logistics shipped 417 million tons of agricultural products in 2017. That's expected to grow to 618 million tons by 2022, and companies like Xianyi Supply Chain and ZM Logistics are poised to grow with it.

Seed companies like Bayer CropScience are also a good bet. Their advantage lies not just in their vast library of seeds, but their scientific approach to developing new products. And while the aquaculture market is still new and fragmented, insect breeders like Protix will profit handsomely from providing fish food to the fish farmers.

The German life sciences company Bayer AG is in an excellent position here. Bayer CropScience is a global operation with sales of more than 14 billion euros in 2018. Its acquisition of Monsanto in 2018 increased its sales by nearly 50 percent and gave it a commanding position in genetically modified seeds and herbicide resistant crops. Monsanto was famous for bringing a biotechnological viewpoint to agriculture, an approach that is compatible with Bayer's own roots as a pharmaceutical company.

After all, there's a lot more to biotechnology than medicine. As the low-hanging clinical targets hit a hard economic wall, entrepreneurs and venture capitalists will gravitate toward new applications of genetic research. We've already seen the first phases of this with veterinary medicine and enhanced livestock feeds, and I think new forms of agricultural products are the next step.

After all, every crop on the planet currently derives from living cells. So do a wide range of essential animal products: wool, dairy, eggs, honey, and even materials like meat, leather, and fur, which can't really be sourced in cruelty-free environments. Within this century, we'll be able to develop microscopic organisms that can produce similar substances on an industrial scale. And we can invest today in companies like Intrexon that are taking the first steps toward making it happen.

XON doesn't make synthetic meat, but it has worked out systems that make existing livestock healthier, more productive, and more nutritious without resorting to artificial hormones or other chemical enhancement. It's a small part of the company's broader ambitions, but doubling the world's sustainable salmon supply is already a prospect. Other products, such as non-browning apples, eliminate "cosmetic" waste and open up new processing approaches.

Other leaders in this sector include the Chinese-owned Syngenta AG and the recent DowDupont spinoff Corteva Agriscience. These companies have global reach, hefty balance sheets, and a broad array of herbicides, fungicides, and seed lines on the market. They also have the scientific and biotechnological culture to develop new product lines and bring them to market.

All three companies are land-based. As powerful as they are in agriculture, they have only a small presence in aquaculture. The global aquaculture market is wide open to new competitors, and fisheries and algae farms represent a true blue ocean market.

The leaders of the aquaculture industry are still best categorized as nations rather than corporations. By this measurement, China is the runaway leader, producing 63 million metric tons of aquatic flora and fauna for human consumption in 2016. That's four times the production of second-ranked Indonesia, more than ten times that of third-ranked India, and more than the entire rest of the world's production of aquaculture in 2012.

Much of that production comes from small fisheries and farms. Despite its outsize aquaculture production, China had only six companies among the one hundred largest seafood companies listed by Undercurrent News in 2018. Japan dominated that list, with twenty-three companies in the top one hundred, though Japan produces only 1.1 million metric tons of aquaculture products per year.

Since there are no dominant players on the field, almost any company could make a breakthrough and become a major player in aquaculture. That company could come from almost anywhere—but the odds favor its being from China.

Don't count the Golden Arches out as a world food leader, either. Throughout its history, McDonalds has played a huge role in shaping the U.S. agriculture industry. It is the biggest buyer of beef in the United States, accounting for about 3 percent of the entire country's consumption. When McDonalds began buying frozen french fries from Simplot in the late 1960s, it changed how potatoes were grown across the country. Today, almost every potato on the market fits the specifications established by McDonalds decades ago.

McDonalds still relies heavily on America's traditional agricultural products: beef, potatoes, and whatever a McRib actually contains. As long as the company holds on to beef, beef is likely to retain a strong hold on American and world palates. But if the company makes a leap into new products—the McVegan, a fish burger, even an algae burger—world food production will follow. The contents of the 2025 Happy Meal will be the go-to comfort food for the adults of 2050.

On that front, brisk capital appreciation also could come from companies like Beyond Meat, but we'll just have to see. I don't believe in novelty for its own sake. Beyond Meat offers plant-based protein substitutes, but a new report found dieticians are not convinced the company's products are much healthier than red meat.

Did you know that old-fashioned General Mills was a major early-stage investor in Beyond Meat and, unlike the startup, it pays a 3.6 percent dividend? Indeed, General Mills offers exposure to the vegetarian burger buzz, none of the volatility, plus double what buy-and-hold index funds have earned since September.

Don't rule out Kellogg, either. That company owns a huge soy burger operation already. Kellogg is at the heart of the new food revolution and offers a 4 percent dividend yield.

Unintended Consequences

Even with the support of McDonalds, the global beef industry has some tough sledding ahead of it. Hamburgers and steaks are delicious, but that may not be enough to keep them on the menu in 2050. In 2017, the U.S. beef industry brought back its old tagline: "Beef. It's what's for dinner." That may still be true today, but in a world where a company like Beyond Meat goes huge, it's already starting to look like wishful thinking.

Beef is a perfect storm of dietary and environmental complaints. While studies have shown that consuming a few ounces of lean red meat per day has no harmful effect on health, that's not the way Americans eat beef. The fatty slabs of meat that we like on our plates have been linked to heart disease, obesity, cancer, strokes, diabetes, even acne.

Pollution is also a serious problem for the beef industry. Cattle are a large source of greenhouse gases, and the deforestation necessary for grazing lands reduces the ecosystem's ability to absorb them. Beef production generates up to 105 grams of greenhouse gases per hundred grams of meat; a similar weight of tofu generates onlys 3.5 grams of greenhouse gases.

Greenhouse gases aren't the only environmental and health hazards associated with beef. Untreated effluence poisons land and water supplies. High consumption of antibiotics is helping breed generations of antibiotic resistant bacteria.

Even if these concerns are addressed, beef production remains incredibly inefficient. It takes twenty-five kilograms of grain and fifteen thousand liters of water to produce one kilogram of beef. A 2018 study showed that meat and dairy production use 83 percent of farmland while providing just 18 percent of the calories and 37 percent of the protein. Abandoning meat and dairy would dramatically increase the food supply while putting a major dent in pollution and climate change.

The world will not go vegan, of course. But beef is so much less efficient than pork, poultry, or fish—never mind exotic alternatives like insects and algae! Beef is a natural first target in improving yields and reducing environmental impact.

Shifting diets are also likely to shake up the fast food industry. McDonalds isn't going away any time soon, but American fast food companies achieved global domination by selling a version of the American diet that is now changing rapidly. That diet is heavy on corn-fed beef, fat, and salt—all problems in a world food culture that is moving toward healthier, plant-based food.

American fast food companies have the buying power to push for changes in what their suppliers offer, but they may not have enough brand power to sell their customers on veggie burgers and seaweed chips. It's a Catch-22. The cheap, popular food that fast food companies offer will become less popular because of health and environmental concerns, while the companies' reputations for being cheap and unhealthy will tarnish any healthier, greener items that they add to their menus.

The strongest American fast food brands will survive. But second-tier brands like Jack in the Box, Pizza Hut, and even Burger King are already struggling. Life is not going to get any easier for them as the global diet changes, and they are likely to be replaced by new food service brands from around the world. Fast food conglomerates like YUM Brands are also on shaky ground. Their reputations as providers of cheap, empty calories will work against them in a food market that is moving toward new and diverse food sources and flavors.

Not every food innovation is going to fly, though. Insects make great meals for fish, but "entopreneurs" like Chapul and Jurassic Snacks are unlikely to build more than a niche audience for cricket bars and enhanced peanut butter. The Western palate may be ready for Beyond Meat veggie burgers, but we won't be dining on bug burgers any time soon.

The Bottom Line for Early Adopters

Food is essential. It's valued at $5 trillion and touches the lives of everyone on earth. That's almost impossible to comprehend, much less interact with in a meaningful way, but there are key areas that will grow quickly as food production evolves.

AI's role in agriculture is growing as farmers deploy machine learning, drone analytics, and robots to grow crops and monitor their livestock. This market was estimated at $518.7 million in 2017 and is expected to reach $2.6 billion by 2025. This market is in turn part of a larger set of practices known as "precision farming," which focuses on reducing waste and getting the most efficient yields from crops and livestock.

Aquaculture is also becoming a big player. The overall market—90 percent of which is devoted to food—was valued at $169 billion in 2015 and is likely to reach $275 billion in 2025. The global commercial seaweeds market alone is projected to reach $23.8 billion by 2025, a compound annual growth rate of 7.9 percent over seven years.

Our relationship with food has changed many times over the centuries. The discovery of agriculture revolutionized human life, turning us from wanderers to settlers and marking the beginnings of civilization. The exploration of the New World introduced new staples like potatoes and tomatoes to the European diet, as well as new luxuries like chocolate.

The Industrial Revolution changed our relationship with food in a way not seen since the invention of agriculture itself. Two hundred years ago, more than 90 percent of Americans lived on farms and produced their own food. Today, just 2 percent of the world's population produces food for everyone. Industrial agriculture has let humanity urbanize and specialize in new arts and sciences. It has also consumed vast quantities of natural resources and polluted both land and sea.

The next few decades in food will be more like the discovery of the New World than the agricultural or industrial revolutions. It will be a sea change, in several senses of the phrase. Agriculture will become more productive and efficient. Aquaculture will play an ever-growing role in the world's food supply. New technology and old traditions will be combined to reduce pollution and increase biodiversity. We will cultivate ecosystems rather than individual crops.

We will also learn to eat new things. When chocolate first came to Europe, it was a bitter, alien food served at royal courts. Then it became a popular novelty. Chocolate houses were the hot, new social gathering places of the late seventeenth century, briefly rivaling the up-and-coming institution of coffee houses. Today, chocolate bars are a commonplace snack, easily within the budget and palate of a picky eight year old.

The food of the future will follow the same progression. In most cultures, algae are a garnish, a nutritional supplement, or a novelty snack. But the children of 2050 are likely to consume algae burgers in their Happy Meals. They'll look and taste as much like grass-fed beef as they want.

CHAPTER FIVE

RISE OF THE LEARNING MACHINES: ARTIFICIAL INTELLIGENCE

Artificial intelligence is already here. While science fiction pondered the nature of human thought and issued cautionary tales about the robot uprising, real artificial intelligence came speeding along in the inside lane. Today the AIs are filtering your email for spam, recommending the next product to buy online, and dutifully answering when you ask your phone for directions to the nearest sushi restaurant.

The learning machines have arrived, and we've welcomed their help with open arms. They make life easier. For some, the complexities of modern life would be unbearable without their guidance and support. Either way, with goliaths like Amazon, Google, and Facebook following IBM's lead putting AI to work for the last decade, you could be forgiven for thinking the robot revolution is yesterday's news. In reality, what we've seen so far are parlor tricks compared to the disruption ahead.

Businesses as far removed from Silicon Valley as it gets are waking up to the potential for AI to revolutionize their analytics, workforce management, marketing, and more. As whole sectors like travel and healthcare embrace an AI-driven world, the pace of development won't slow. Full-fledged revolutions like self-driving cars and automated drug discovery are set to change the face of business forever.

Oddly, Star Trek's Commander Data is nowhere to be seen. We have nothing resembling a human-level AI that can tackle philosophical questions about its own existence and befriend a cat. But what AI developers have realized is that for a huge variety of applications, you shouldn't be worrying about whether your code can think like we do. You only need it to *learn* how to solve the problems you set in front of it.

Everything Starts with Big Data

The central idea behind machine learning is simple. Rather than trying to solve a problem from first principles, you build a flexible piece of software that knows how to guess at a solution. It doesn't need to hit the target the first time. It simply needs to make an approximation, evaluate its accuracy, and then try again.

Practice literally makes perfect. Done right, a machine learning system spots patterns and trends in information far more quickly and accurately than a team of human experts—as long as you can keep feeding it relevant information about the problem.

Fortunately, data is something that businesses have in abundance, often far more than their human analysts can keep up with. Big Data has earned its imposing capital letters. This is a resource so intimidatingly huge that your analyst's desktop computer gives up and dies when it tries to work with it, a problem commonly described as trying to "drink from a hosepipe." With enough processing power behind them, an AI can drink from that hosepipe all day long without drowning.

A few years ago, machine learning algorithms were hand-crafted by code artisans with a distinct love for advanced mathematics. But the basic tools of AI are becoming ever more available to a wider range of developers. A neural network (a kind of machine learning tool based on the way the human brain works) can be put together by anyone in less than an hour.

There are open source code libraries, such as Google's TensorFlow, which offer these tools for free. Amazon Web Services, NVIDIA, and others offer AI as a service in the cloud. Now that the tools are widely available, we can expect the endless application of machine learning, from facial recognition to predictive analytics to robotics, to grow rapidly. It won't be long before processor chips specially designed to handle AI processing are on the market.

Hollywood has warned us to keep a watchful eye on our AI helpers, but the reality is that our AI helpers will be keeping an eye on us. Fraud detection, which relies on spotting subtle patterns in past transactions, is an ideal arena for machine learning. By simply flagging data points that don't match normal spending patterns, AI could save banks endless effort and money, if not stop credit card scamming entirely.

It's certainly true that the sheer power of these predictive systems will always tempt unscrupulous data miners illicitly to capture information about your behavior and use it to exploit your habits. People have resisted the urge to log in to Facebook, for example, and raised valid privacy concerns. But there are more guardians than renegades: AIs already police each other.

We need this AI auto-policing because when you're handling eye-bleeding quantities of Big Data, simply keeping user information private at ground level is a vast and complex job. Practically speaking, humans can't do it without help from AI. Obviously we do still need to remain in the loop to make judgement calls about how user data should be used and what patterns the systems should chase.

At the operational level, ensuring compliance is itself a Big Data problem. Crucial institutions like banks and hospitals now operate as pattern-driven environments, with machine learning systems reporting infractions of the rules. The rules aren't always inflexible. Someone with authority can usually override the pattern to allow an exception. Too many exceptions can then create a pattern of their own for human investigators to evaluate.

After all, while the Big Data universe will usually obey statistical laws, individual situations always have the potential to bend the probability curve. Machine learning systems only see the rules. Human beings navigate a world of exceptions in which we pursue individual objectives and look to creative outlets to relieve boredom.

Think of an automated telephone customer service system. At every level, you're provided with a menu of options programmed to capture and route as many calls as possible. When your problem fits those parameters, the process is painless. Otherwise, you're forced to find a big enough loophole to exit the menu and get another human on the line. This system is a great example of the machine learning interface. It resolves as many calls as possible according to its rules before deploying precious and expensive human expertise.

But as you know, the phone menu has no mercy. It isn't very good at hearing the exasperation in your voice. That's our job.

Automation: An Inside Job

Not all our artificial allies inhabit our phones like Siri. Manufacturing is already a heavily automated industry, but until recently, each robotic assembly line was built to follow a fixed set of procedures. When the factory needed to shift to a new production profile, those machines had to be ripped out and completely reconfigured.

It was slow, inflexible, and ultimately expensive. Cutting edge factories will soon have robotic assembly units that can adjust to changing circumstances more nimbly. Their machines will be able to learn. Simply tell them *what* to build, and they'll figure out *how* on their own.

Robots in factories and warehouses can already "see" the objects they're manipulating by means of the same kinds of onboard cameras that alert taxi drivers to potential obstacles in their collision zones. When they see what they need, they reach for it. And when they see a problem, they compensate right away, without waiting for the quality control team to come around and notice that hours' or days' worth of work need to be redone or thrown out.

The factory of 2050 won't be specialized. Much like today's global supply contracts, all the manufacturer needs is a design in a format the system can understand and the right raw materials. When the order is ready, other systems pack the pieces into a shipping crate and signal an automated pickup to take it where it needs to go. Meanwhile, the factory will already have shifted gears to process the next order. One day, it might be basketballs. Another day, global retailers may decide they need more desk chairs. The production line will be able to keep moving with minimal downtime in between.

Once the factories are running, the only constraints will be the library of processes they "know" and the raw materials in their inventory. 3D printing technology means that more of the supply chain can be manufactured on site rather than transported from a distant manufacturer. This is opening up a world of on-demand local production where a customer can send a 3D design file to the nearest production center, where the design will be executed and shipped the minute the machines are ready. There's no warehouse. Everything will be built to order, from components to packaging.

The Holographic House Call

The same kinds of machine learning algorithms that can scan financial records for possible fraudulent transactions can also be applied to medical scans. These images never even need to be printed because the scanner itself knows the difference between a healthy colon and something that requires additional tests. And because the system never sleeps, chronic conditions can be monitored and flagged instantly when the symptoms change.

We need more physicians. The training process is long, expensive, and famously difficult. But even after training is completed, there's a lot of room for human error. Hospital personnel get tired but refuse to clock out, or work overtime when the case load piles up. Every diagnostic task an AI can learn from human experts reduces that load, in theory making it possible for both physicians and patients to live healthier lives without spending a fortune.

The model is preventative screening. Sign up for regular scans and let the system evaluate the results according to guidelines the best human doctors have developed. It's like having the Mayo Clinic monitor your heart. In fact, the monitoring may even be done according to Mayo Clinic protocols for everyone in the system, no matter where we live or how many of us there are.

Most of the time, the scans will come up negative, and the system will move on to the next test. If there is anything a human doctor would find concerning, it would trigger a referral. Ambiguous cases will be flagged for a second opinion and follow-up tests. Initially, there will be a lot of these edge cases, but as scanners learn from experience built up from past tests, accuracy will quickly improve.

Doctors will spend their time working with sick people. You will have a much better sense of your health at all times. And because automated diagnostics are cheaper and simpler than full-fledged intervention, more resources will be available to review false positives and catch problems as early as possible, when they are easier to address.

Remote and automated procedures will expand the reach of a gifted surgeon's skills. At least initially, the doctor will monitor the robots' work, as if the robots were conventional interns who might need expert assistance if things get complicated. Sooner or later, that world-class specialist will be available by robot proxy in every clinic big enough to buy the machine and rent the program.

That's a good thing in my book. The robots can make mistakes, but so can human surgeons. If the surgeons license their expertise, more people get better, no matter where they live. Automatic drug dispensers can identify and dispense pills with fewer errors and better security than human pharmacists can provide. Even the process of drug development can be partially automated through Big Data systems that can scan millions of molecules to find the right fit for any given condition.

Of course there are some who won't be eager to entrust their health to computer programs they usually associate with screening email and correcting spelling. But if we learned to trust doctors, food inspectors, and airline pilots, we should be able to acquire confidence here, too.

An AI will never truly understand the underlying medical principles separating life and death, health and sickness. All it can do is evaluate data as instructed and then follow the procedures it was given. Even so, when that diagnostic system can review millions of test results without getting tired, that brute power will transform the world. When wearable sensors feed a patient's results back to the system on a regular basis, nobody will slip through the cracks.

Let Siri Cut through the Noise

The core benefits of AI are speed, volume, and accuracy. The larger the system scales, the more cost-effective it is, and because more data points are available in larger systems, the AI has more opportunities to get smarter. A well-programmed machine learning system doesn't get sloppy as it grows; it actually improves, freeing up other resources to work on exceptional cases.

The same cannot be said for humans. Self-driving cars can suffer network failure, but they never get drunk, stressed, or fall asleep. The most dedicated professional will perform inconsistently according to fluctuations in mental and physical health, sleep cycle, mood, and even what they had for lunch. The AI will perform at the same level every time.

Now, machines are learning to take over the majority of repetitive tasks, so tomorrow's human workforce will deal primarily with the unique, the ambiguous, and the unexpected. Everything else will yield to automation. Don't let this scare you. If you do a lot of repetitive work, you've spent a lot of your life trying to be like a robot. It's time to let an actual robot take over the routine, freeing you to do what you actually do best. Humans are great at dealing with ambiguity, solving problems, and dealing with one-of-a-kind issues. We enjoy it. Automation will allow us to focus on the more challenging and stimulating areas of our work, which allow us to exercise the distinctly human qualities of judgment and creativity.

Admittedly, this transition will not be easy. Some estimates suggest that half of the jobs that exist today will be automated by 2050. And automation reaches far beyond self-driving vehicles and robotic warehouses. While doctors and lawyers will never be replaced *en masse* by computers, it will become possible for a single professional to be more productive without an entire staff of various assistants, clerks, typists, and receptionists.

The ongoing AI transformation is sure to disrupt many areas of industry. One of the first casualties will be call centers. AI chatbots using machine learning algorithms can observe and learn from queries that human operators currently process. The number of humans required to field routine questions has already dropped to the point where everyone you end up talking to will soon be an expert in making you feel better while solving genuinely new or unique customer support challenges. They'll be your corporate therapists, talking you through your corporate problems.

Then there's banking, where accounts are already monitored more closely than ever. Discrepancies are caught and referred to managers in real time. And systems are watching your cash flow. Machine learning software can match market trends to customer behavior in a blink of an eye and adjust financial marketing tactics accordingly. Has it been a few years since your last car loan? Would you benefit from a mortgage refinancing or a specialized credit card? Have you used your debit card in Florida a lot lately? You'll get relevant offers.

Getting Disruption on Your Side

Much of the groundbreaking work is being done behind the scenes by the familiar tech giants. IBM, of course, has Big Blue systems available for everyone from chess masters to tax accountants. Start there. The scope of the financial opportunity is vast. PwC's Global Artificial Intelligence Study projected that AI will contribute $15.7 trillion to the world economy by 2030, and 45 percent of these gains will come from product enhancements that will stimulate customer demand.

A key idea here is that AI will lead to a greater variety of products, with vast potential for personalization and affordable alternatives. Matching those products to customers will be the challenge of the future. The cloud computing giant Salesforce commissioned a report from the International Data Corporation which found that AI in this field will lead to a $1.1 trillion revenue boost by 2021 and 800,000 *new* jobs in excess of those lost to automation.

Alphabet, Google's parent conglomerate, is heavily invested in this technology in order to make ads more responsive to individual patterns of interest. Whenever you click one site from a list of search results or let the browser bar complete your search terms for you, you're helping that system learn. Fun toys like the "Deep Dream" picture manipulation tools actually teach the company's image recognition systems to think visually the way you do, paving the way to targeted ads that run on pictures as well as words.

And Google is rapidly becoming more than the search engine. Back in 2014, Alphabet bought DeepMind, a London startup that has already developed a way to aggregate key medical information, like blood test results, and notify physicians if any patient's condition takes a turn for the worse. The UK's National Health Service is testing the app now.

Amazon is automating too. Forget the warehouses populated with robots: a trial deployment of eleven AI-enabled convenience stores has already begun in four cities, with plans to ramp up to a 3,000-store chain by 2021. An app lets you through the door, and then the system tracks your movements as you fill your own shopping bag. There's no checkout counter. Take what you want and walk out, knowing that the app will add up your purchases and charge your account. It costs about $1 million right now to set up a single store, but at $1.5 million a year in sales, that investment will pay off fast.

Silicon Valley household names are well and good, but investors hoping for higher-impact opportunities should look down the AI food chain to smaller companies working on specific applications. Take Twilio, the integrated communications platform that runs Facebook and Uber messaging apps. What few realize is that the system also gives enterprising customers a way to build and manage cutting-edge chatbots to automate the majority of their customer service needs, effectively taking the humans right out of the communications loop.

When corporations need to protect themselves from being taken advantage of by their own customers, they may turn to Signifyd, a Seattle startup founded in 2011, which is now the world's largest provider of guaranteed fraud prevention. The system automatically reviews online purchasing patterns and tells retailers whether to ship each order or not, reducing the financial drag of fraudulent transactions and chargebacks. Signifyd is so confident in their AI that they offer a financial guarantee on all transactions the app approves.

Landing AI is another startup to watch, not least because of the pedigree of its founder. Andrew Ng, former chief scientist at Baidu, was at Google Brain and online learning platform Coursera from the beginning. He's probably the most influential scholar of machine learning in the world. His own Coursera course on the topic remains the go-to for those wanting to learn about AI algorithms and neural networks. Now he's working to bring the benefits of this technology to executives well beyond Silicon Valley. Landing AI provides consulting for manufacturing organizations in particular.

That's probably where the money will go between now and 2050. As in any gold rush, the real wealth doesn't go to the miners. It ends up with the people who sell prospecting tools. Where AI is concerned, we are probably past the point where fundamental advances will yield huge profits and besides, none of today's dominant players offer anything like pure exposure to the theme.

Alphabet is a search advertising company with a side of machine learning. IBM is a full-spectrum technology solutions provider that incorporates AI into its consulting operations. Amazon is evaluated according to how much stuff it sells, even if automated systems pick the products and seal the boxes. And with many machine learning algorithms available via open source code libraries, the tools are available to anyone with vision and a good business plan.

I would avoid the traditional tech sector entirely here. Focus on consulting firms and system integrators, the people building the targeted applications that will unlock explosive margin expansion for early adopters and stunning income opportunities for the rest of us. Don't ask how smart the programmers are. Focus on the sales team. Who's talking to the doctors about licensing their surgical techniques? The AI revolution in healthcare will require the trust of the public, so seek out companies who are looking to build that trust.

Unintended Consequences

The biggest hurdle many investors must face is the assumption that, after years of hype, the AI boom to come is already over. This field is a lot like science fiction: it hits first as a dream for a few people chattering on the economic frontier, and then that dream conquers the world. In the middle of the story, a lot of heavy lifting translates into tangible results.

Admittedly, the Silicon Valley-centered experience of buying a laptop online today is suffused with AI from start to finish. But your experience of going to the hospital, for example, has not changed. That is potential that has yet to be realized. There are massive gains to be made in the coming years, in hospitals, in grocery stores, in fitness centers, in pharmacies, and beyond. Until that happens, progress will be scattered and there will be times that it will feel grindingly slow.

It is incumbent on the business leaders of today and tomorrow to find ways to seamlessly integrate the brute power and consistency of automation with the imagination and agility of human thought. There needs to be space for human intervention. Otherwise, nobody's going to be happy, and temporary backlash will slow adoption.

Another factor to be wary of is that many corporate leaders do not yet see the business case for adopting AI. Particularly where Big Data "insights" are concerned, the long-term benefits may seem nebulous, while deployment costs are high. Companies that spend too much time arguing with skeptical executives will squander whatever first-mover advantage they have. The systems may be excellent but if nobody can recognize the concrete application immediately, the businesses behind them will starve.

Again, it takes time for machines to learn any business. Only humans lose patience and cancel programs with vast potential along the way. That's what investors need to keep in mind here. Diversify your bets and take a long view. Keep it small. Keep it practical. You only need a few of your portfolio companies to leap from dream to giant to generate a reasonable return.

The Bottom Line for Early Adopters

It's difficult to overestimate the impact that machine learning will have on our society. Andrew Ng has compared AI to electricity because it will be a resource deployed across a huge variety of sectors and markets without becoming a predominant industry in itself. Before electricity, people still ate, slept, worked, and played. And after electricity, people still did those things. But the world around them had changed.

We're at the very beginning of the cultural discourse that will allow industrial society to adapt to widespread automation. Work is changing. Does history give us cause to be pessimistic about the reduction in the amount of labor that needs to be done? Not necessarily. Advances in agriculture and commerce in the ancient world created sections of the population with more control over their time and labor.

Think of ancient Greece. We don't think of its citizens as lazy decadents, but rather as philosophers, poets, playwrights, and political visionaries. In the ancient world, citizenship was a privilege of the few. A thousand menial tasks still needed to be performed by hard-working and poorly-compensated members of society. One dream of an automated future is that of universal "citizenship," where the removal of physical and mental drudgery will allow everyone the time and energy to participate fully in intellectual and cultural life.

CHAPTER SIX

The $70 Million Man: Joints, Genes, and Beyond

I love medical research. While individual research programs may be somewhat speculative, the odds of a successful cure for cancer, Alzheimer's disease, diabetes, or any of the other pandemic conditions plaguing modern humanity have never been higher. The relief for suffering populations will be enormous. And for investors in the right place at the right time, the financial rewards will be transformational.

As we say around here, this is where world-changing products are created out of nothing but insight, dedication, and the drive to improve human lives. It takes insight to discover or synthesize an attractive molecule. Then it takes dedication to determine the right dosage, plan the commercial manufacturing process, and prove to regulators that your drug's benefits outweigh any side effects.

The route is precarious. Opportunities abound to lose years of hard-won progress—and billions of shareholder dollars if the clinical data don't line up with your best-laid plans. But when everything works, it's almost miraculous. And right now, we see the stocks working hardest toward transformational therapies which factor in more negativity than hope.

The Skeleton Supports the Brain

Start with the foundation. In the last century innovators, scientists, surgeons, and engineers working together have made massive strides in replacing damaged, deteriorating, or missing parts of the body. From the wooden toes carved in Egypt 3,000 years ago to Elon Musk's proposed brain-computer interface, medical science has come a long way.

And yet the human condition remains as precarious as ever. People lose limbs to war, disease, and accidents. Genetic defects lead to heart conditions and blindness. Bad diets have led to epidemic diabetes and obesity. We find ourselves struggling against the environment and even our own bodies.

Human history began in an unforgiving world where our ancestors rarely lived to see forty, much less fifty. But things are changing fast now. Wonderful drugs reprogram the brain, relieving pain, increasing focus and alertness, even easing our reliance on sleep. Prosthetics respond to thought and let amputees live and function normally. Lightweight "blade runners" even enhance performance beyond the limits of Olympic-level athletes. Eye enhancements through laser surgery correct weak vision, and the blind can see through head-mounted camera images transmitted directly to the brain.

Artificial hips. Artificial hearts. Artificial teeth. As we live longer, we need to replace the parts that wear out first. Most of us are partially cyborg these days, fueling what's already a $125 billion global industry. That's not even counting cosmetic implants some people buy just to look different.

It can be expensive. Replacing all major joints with artificial hardware and organs could cost $70 million—if you can find a donor. Imagine someone paralyzed from birth. State of the art prosthetics like the "Dexterous Hand" developed by Shadow Robot Company make mechanical programming for specific tasks largely obsolete because it can be coupled with the brain. The Dexterous Hand works much like the hands we were born with. After a decade of development, it has twenty-four joints, twenty degrees of freedom, and four under-actuated movements, identical to the range of motion our own hands have. One hundred twenty-nine built-in sensors allow the Dexterous Hand to feel and function exactly as your own hands do now.

Only they're stronger, more coordinated, and much easier to repair or replace. This kind of prosthetic will be particularly useful to people who work in dangerous conditions where losing a hand is not unheard of: mines, oil rigs, large-scale engineering and manufacturing plants, etc.

That's not even mentioning the number of health risks a prosthetic mitigates. A machine, after all, cannot get infected. It needs to be cleaned, but there is no blood flow between the installed unit and the rest of the body, so even heavy damage to it won't translate into serious illness. It isn't vulnerable to contagious disease.

Almost every organ in the human body can be substituted. For instance, the Galveston National Laboratory at the University of Texas recently developed rejection-free, completely safe, and working lungs built specifically for the recipient. Beyond the benefits to the recipients of artical organs, this development will massively reduce trade in human organs. It will simply be less profitable for traffickers to operate.

Augmenting the Brain Itself

Elon Musk has invested $100 million in a "Neuralink" system that implants special fiber optic "communication threads" through the skull and connects them directly to the brain. These threads then read signals that are amplified through a microprocessor. They connect to a computer with a common USB-C cable. (At this point, you're directly immersed in the Internet of Things.)

As with all such cybernetics, the procedure is invasive. Musk envisions a special robot surgeon something like a sewing machine punching tiny holes through the skull to insert six threads a minute. Within roughly a quarter of an hour, the brain is wired. Add a dedicated modem, and you'll never need to type again.

To some of us, it's a vision somewhere between bizarre and horrifying. But give someone with progressive motor neuron disease or another form of paralysis the chance to communicate with useful household robots and other people, and the picture changes. Think of Stephen Hawking, laboriously flexing his cheek to construct every sentence he would "speak" for decades, or any of the people whose brain implants have helped them control robotic arms to feed themselves.

As with so many of the other hyper-disruptive technologies in this book, once the most immediate humanitarian applications exist, it's going to be hard to prevent people from developing new ones. If the contents of the skull can be routed via data cable, there's nothing to stop early-stage dementia patients from finding a way to upload their memories into an archive for later retrieval when storage within the brain itself has failed. Musk hopes the Neuralink system will ultimately support a complete transfer of consciousness into a specially grown or 3-D printed replacement body.

In that scenario, something like immortality is achievable (if you're rich enough and want to treat your body as something disposable when it wears out). I don't, but as I write this, Musk's ideas have already captured their share of attention ahead of the soliciation of what could be the first human volunteer test subjects. Even partial integrations of new parts with old brains can have sweeping ramifications for the way we live, work, and play.

Personalized Medicine

And then there's genetic engineering. Just recently scientists in China reported that they're starting trials for an HIV vaccine on 160 human volunteers. The vaccine is called DNA-rTV and relies on the replication of the viral strain's DNA, thus cutting down on its impact when the patient is infected with the real thing. Chinese scientists are hopeful that these second-phase trials will be completed in the second half of 2021.

Gene therapy theoretically opens up some of the most transformative benefits of biotech medicine by repairing or replacing errors in the genetic code. These errors can include inherited blindness and other hereditary conditions as well as mutations that trigger cancer and other fatal diseases. Fixing the errant gene eliminates the problem at the source.

However, genetic disorders tend to be rare in the general population, which means fewer potential patients to amortize development costs. In general, the rarer your condition, the higher the bills you—or your insurance company—will be asked to pay.

On the surface, it's a classic all-or-nothing binary proposition: if the science works, the company that invested in its development can improve the human condition and build a profitable business at the same time. Otherwise, the time and money are wasted. In the first scenario, shareholders make money. In the second, they're out of luck.

Right now, the economies of scale on some of these therapies only make sense on the order of a million dollars or more per treatment. That's what the only one currently on the market costs to cure a rare blood disease that affects maybe 28,000 people worldwide. It's a fantastic technology that truly cures the underlying enzyme deficiency, which means that after 28,000 of those million dollar shots, the disease has been eradicated in the current population and the revenue window closes.

Needless to say, that's a big immediate price tag for each patient, though it means the difference between life and death. It raises huge questions about financing arrangements, sustainable revenue, and the ultimate economic value of an individual.

Getting Disruption on Your Side

As these companies force answers to these questions, pricing structures will evolve one way or another. If they don't, regulatory approval doesn't really even matter—from a long-term investment perspective, a successful drug or experimental orthopedic implant you can't sell on a profitable basis is worth as much as one that simply doesn't work well enough to get through the FDA process in the first place.

That's where I invest. With very few exceptions, only the ten biggest biotech companies are profitable, and they're very big, easily accounting for 50 percent of all the capital circulating in the industry. They're really more like Big Pharma, mature and facing either fierce competition or looming patent expirations. Every day without breakthroughs brings them closer to that "patent cliff."

Their most disruptive days are behind them. That's why I look behind the index for smaller opportunities where a little good news can transform a balance sheet that's otherwise built out of little more than hope. I love the smaller companies in developmental stages with little to no sales or earnings. They're speculative, forcing Wall Street to evaluate them on the probability that their science will one day turn into money and a sustainable business. I buy these companies based on the odds that they'll change the world.

And remember, mergers and acquisitions are a fact of life in this industry as large players facing that patent cliff buy out their more innovative counterparts before they can grow into bona fide competitors. I've seen a lot of favorite biotech stocks taken out for cash over the years. That's going to continue. But in the meantime, there are over 500 ambitious little companies on the market today with big dreams. The ones aiming at the right target will change the world. The others will keep trying until they run out of cash.

One more thing about biotech. These aren't giants yet. This is not a mature business—like email or web search or smartphones for that matter. While the industry has a dedicated following on Wall Street, the stocks haven't gotten the huge rush of capital that Big Tech has. Think of Silicon Valley in 1996 or 1997. Big money hasn't come in here yet to push up valuations before the IPO even happens.

But sometimes a little maturity is good. Uber is supposedly a $70 billion company. It's not profitable. Practically nothing in biotech can match that size except Amgen, which easily does 60 percent more sales than Uber even dreams of and turns 40 percent of it into profit. If you can buy into one $70 billion stock, Amgen has the edge. It's big. It's relatively mature. But Uber already has 70 percent of the ride share market sewn up, and it's only booking fourteen billion a year in sales. Amgen can grow as long as we're not happy with our health.

And that means the company is probably looking at a long growth curve ahead. Of course I wouldn't recommend Amgen right now until we see new programs start pushing the envelope. More likely it's going to buy a few rivals first. Did I mention Amgen has $29 billion in cash? That's enough to buy two top-ten biotech companies and absorb their growth. That's how this industry works. Little stocks come and go. They turn into big ones, which themselves ultimately get absorbed into the entrenched Big Pharma universe.

My favorites are the ones that focus on cures for significant medical problems rather than spending their resources making healthy people healthier. Their management teams pick their targets carefully and lay out careful, strategic plans to get their therapies past the FDA. The pharmaceutical market for epilepsy, for example, is small but growing at a steady 4 percent per year. There should be $5.4 billion a year here by 2024.

That's a good enough opportunity for an emerging developer like GW Pharmaceuticals to chase.

GWPH is looking to expand the size of this market by seeking orphan status for its products, meaning it can treat diseases that are serious in nature but neglected by larger pharmaceutical firms that would see a significant impact to their bottom line. When drugs are granted orphan status, companies are given tax credits to research costs to develop them and are protected from any competition for seven years.

We're going to get into the science a bit here, which will include the accompanying scientific terminology, but I really want you to understand the potential with GWPH. The company's flagship product is Epidiolex, which got a green light from the FDA in 2018 and is now ramping up sales while follow-up trials move toward pinning down the drug's ability to fight rare tumors and other conditions.

While the near-term success of the company will depend on how wide a patient population Epidiolex can capture, there are other drugs in the pipeline that GWPH would like to get in front of the FDA soon. Cannabidivarin, or CBDV, is in Phase II development for epilepsy and is also being researched within the field of autism spectrum disorders. In addition, the company has received Orphan Drug Designation and Fast Track Designation from the FDA for the treatment of Neonatal Hypoxic Ischemic Encephalopathy (NHIE). The loss of oxygen in newborns stemming from NHIE is a major cause of cerebral palsy. Any of these therapies will change lives.

I'm not a fan of medical device developers working on implants that expand healthy people's capabilities while so many others need more help before they can live independently, without pain or constant medical intervention. Abiomed, a company that has seen extraordinary growth in recent years from its Impella line of heart pumps, is rarely far from my radar. Impella's small size enables high-risk patients to have angioplasty and other procedures that may not have been an option previously. It's exactly what I look to medical stocks to provide.

And on that note, with 900 healthcare companies trading on Wall Street, most of them are usually on my screen one way or another. Each in its way is working to heal the sick.

Unintended Consequences

Maybe you love having a tablet or voice-operated computer always close at hand, ready to translate your gestural commands and spoken words into action. At a minimum, the assistant answers your questions, automates your daily routines, and acts as a concierge, smoothing the way you interact with the world around you.

Now maybe you love that computer so much that you want to bring the interface inside the body. Bypassing the physical medium of typing is going to massively improve productivity in every way, provided of course that you measure productivity in terms of the amount of information you can access and manipulate. Imagine being able to learn any language you wanted in a single evening. Or what if you wanted to learn everything there is to know about the history of World War II?

As with cybernetic implants motivated by performance instead of medical necessity, the looming reality of genetic therapy raises the prospect that some parents will enhance their children to get ahead. At which point do we decide which devices and which enhancements are unfair? Athletes with light and powerful artificial legs can run in the Olympics. Can a singer with an augmented throat win a Grammy?

It's up to us to decide where to draw the line between the limits of elective surgery and applications that serve a medical purpose. We'll need to redefine what we consider "healthy." I suspect that won't be legislated. Community standards will once again determine who stretches their bodily presentation too far or who cheats nature to get ahead (or simply to get noticed). We already make our children turn off their phones and calculators when they're taking a test. One day, some schools will make the kids turn off the implants their parents bought them.

I don't know how they'll turn off their genes. We might end up in a world where the rich truly are better looking because their parents could afford the best genes. They'll be healthier, disease-free, more athletic, more musical. In that respect, the future will look a lot like the past. The only difference will be that we'll finally have ways to give a better deal to those who weren't dealt such a great hand from birth. They'll have a chance to see, walk, talk, dance—as long as the insurance companies can find a way to pay the bills, of course.

The Bottom Line for Early Adopters

We haven't even touched on the companies that are trying to cure aging itself. That's a long way away, but until that day, our bodies will decline sooner or later despite all our best efforts. It's part of the human condition. Medicine will only be a mature industry when (and more likely if) all the pain points are cured once and for all. While I don't envision that happening, there's always room for improvement.

Medicine will never make us perfect. Every new cure does more than incrementally boost productivity and improve lives. It saves lives. It's the difference between nothing and something, life and death. And there are so many targets that no single company could hope to cure them all, even in a profoundly enhanced and extended lifetime.

This is where medical miracles happen. Medical miracles cost money but investors lucky enough to put their money on the right programs can get rewards here like nowhere else.

CHAPTER SEVEN

DIGITAL BULLION: THE FUTURE OF MONEY

Bitcoin may be the talk of Main Street lately, but Wall Street is all about "fintech," the marriage of finance and technology. That's bitcoin and other crypto currencies that only exist inside computer screens, but that's only the tip of the fintech iceberg. Fintech is the payment systems that render the credit card obsolete and cash mysterious to today's kids. It's the new, automated approaches to banking, insurance, lending, and even investing. Stretch your definition, and it's the new ways to buy and sell real estate and other assets without a broker.

And if you weren't around for the early, meteoric days of bitcoin, don't worry. There's innovation on the horizon that will make that bonanza look pitifully small. I'm talking about a $1 trillion opportunity, as big as the money all the FAANG giants (Facebook, Amazon, Apple, Netflix, and Google) make together. It's the foundation of an all-new Internet that's safer, more efficient, and scalable to accommodate billions of devices. I'm talking about blockchain.

Some revolutions start as distant rumbles and take years before the vibrations start rocking Wall Street. That's the stage where this technological breakthrough is now. I've had an eye on this computational technique for a while now—but at long last, commercial applications are ready for prime time and in a place where retail investors can start capturing a piece of the action.

The Chain behind the Coin

Strip away the jargon, and blockchain boils down to a way to authenticate transactions within a cloud of networked computers. There's so much processing power built into each link in the data "chain" that it's practically impossible to break the code. Only computers with legitimate access can authorize any activity whatsoever. Everyone else is locked out. And if anyone tries to tamper with the chain, the deception is obvious to all.

It's a cybersecurity system that enforces itself. And that self-enforcing structure allows networks backed with blockchain to replace the conventional Internet, ultimately raising serious questions about the future of money itself.

Anyone with an eye on financial markets knows about bitcoin now, as what was worth one dollar a decade ago occasionally trades for well over $10,000. But what they may not know is that the digital-only currency runs on blockchain systems that verify custody of every microscopic fraction of digital money. Those same systems back up the entire currency in much the same way a central bank would, guaranteeing transactions with the full faith and credit of the network's processing power while eliminating forgery and fraud.

Nobody who's paying attention will ever buy a fake bitcoin because they'll always be able to confirm that the seller is telling the truth or detect that he's lying. It's that simple. Instead of all the special inks and secret printing tricks that authenticate modern currency, the numbers do all the work.

If You Like the Coin, You'll Love the Chain

While I think the cryptocurrency story is far from over, its mushrooming popularity means that the easy gains will have played out by the time Wall Street unveils mutual funds and other vehicles designed to lower the obstacles that currently make it hard for retail investors to play. It's still a rarefied trade for relative experts. When it's as easy to exchange for dollars as a handful of yen or euros, it will simply be another form of money.

But where this gets exciting is in the multiplication of new currencies, each supported by its own blockchain and its own parameters of value. In just the last few months, we've seen bitcoin split across several new networks in order to make room for expanded trading volume and user preference. As each version evolves, some will become more valuable while others deteriorate. Meanwhile, independent alternatives are emerging around a competing source of value: gold coins, diamonds, and even old-fashioned nation states.

This will get extremely interesting as more and more physical objects are associated into the blockchain universe (I'll discuss one commodity in particular in just a moment). For now, while we may be in the fourth inning of the bitcoin story, we've only thrown the first pitch on digital currencies in general.

The Unhackable Planet

As we discussed in Chapter Two, the "things" around us are increasingly going to be smart, network-enabled devices that can communicate with each other. We've already seen how easy the first generation of smart refrigerators and televisions are to hack. If it's the television, losing control of the device is just a nuisance.

Medical devices, home security systems, and yes, even cars are more vulnerable to truly malicious interference. They require better security. When I went to experts to tell me who had the best systems to protect our power grid and vital infrastructure, they practically started to cry.

Since blockchain is the best security protocol around, it's the logical choice for locking down the evolving Internet of Things. You can give authorized guests an electronic key to your smart house that runs on blockchain permissions that you set—maybe it expires for short-term visitors, maybe it only works on a set schedule for deliveries or service calls.

Blockchain will protect your autonomous car from being taken over on the road and rammed into oncoming traffic. If the hackers don't have the right codes, they can't override the system or feed the car's brain faulty navigational data. Needless to say, blockchain will (or at least should) restrict electronic access to military equipment, critical infrastructure, and even sensitive corporate property.

This applies to virtual property as well. Blockchain can protect network space better than any commercial security system currently on the market. There will always be hackers, but cracking this code is already difficult and expensive. For most everyday targets, it's unlikely to be worth the effort.

And this is true throughout the fintech universe. Fintech is as hot as it gets, all over the world. All it takes right now to make venture capitalists open their checkbooks is an entrepreneurial attitude, a business plan, and a vision that applies technology to financial services. Solutions providers with an integrated financial focus have a strategic edge in today's marketplace. Last year alone, investors pushed a record $39 billion at start-ups that automate everything from nickel-and-dime cash transfers to all the intricacies of running an elite family office.

From the financial side, adding a slice of tech to your profile gives you an essential edge. A little nomenclature makes a huge difference when it comes to the enterprise value of your business. But that tech needs to be secure because money is by definition purchasing power, which every financial institution makes as difficult as possible to steal. You don't want the bank to get hacked, even if it's a next-generation account on a website or a special store credit card that people in emerging economies use online.

That's where the chain shines. The encryption is theoretically perfect. These accounts can't be cracked, and from a privacy point of view they're as good as it gets.

No Litigation Required

Professional relationships are transactional. Blockchain validates transactions. I'm hearing talk about blockchain enabling smart contracts that enforce themselves: if one party defaults, the code works behind the scenes to unwind the transaction or negotiate penalties. When our devices can argue amongst each other on our behalf, we'll know the future has arrived.

And somewhere between digital reality and legal reality, intellectual property is a staggering but largely invisible slice of the "real" global economy. Patents, copyrights, and trademarks need to be protected, and violations need to be enforced. Kodak is working on a way to embed blockchain code into commercial photographs. Reproduce that image without clearing the licensing rights, and the code will negotiate payment or simply prohibit access.

Now apply that approach to songs, movies, and other streaming content. The Hollywood of 2050 will be free from piracy... unless future pirates somehow find a way around "unbreakable" encryption. Wherever the applications go, Goldman Sachs is arguably the leader, selling capabilities to other institutions willing to embrace the future. These guys are already the smartest ones in the room, but their leadership in blockchain for financial institutions proves that they're not asleep at the wheel.

Getting Disruption on Your Side

Every digital transaction feeds the blockchain ecosystem, starving conventional transaction networks that protect participants via signature, PIN, or other validation techniques. Those networks are ultimately going to need to buy or build blockchain capabilities to remain relevant.

And they're all going to need computing power. That's the first piece of the opportunity. IBM has the early lead on the programming to give would-be blockchain vendors a plug-and-play franchise, while NVIDIA and AMD make the chips that keep running the numbers. Alphabet has a front-row seat on the start-up end of the industry with a half-dozen interesting little companies in the portfolio. These aren't pure plays, but they'll catch the buzz.

You may think it's a bit of a jump to go from digital transactions to small business, but hear me out. Depending on the day, there's maybe $120 billion packed into the bitcoin universe, and it's taken a decade to get there. Right now, small e-commerce vendors generate about $160 billion a year in sales for Amazon and another $40 million a year for Shopify. Ordinarily, we'd suspect a lot of that merchandise was pirated or simply never existed.

What's exciting about this application of blockchain systems is that in theory any commodity, product, or even service can be linked to the line of transactions that represent its economic history. I've seen presentations from people who are building "smart" concert and sporting event tickets that are impossible to forge or scalp. If you try to break the embedded rules of resale, the ticket itself warns the buyer and could even alert the authorities.

The prescription angle can theoretically help stamp out opioid and other addictions by locking each pill bottle to the person who legitimately needs the medicine—while the pills themselves can still be traded or stolen, they can't be resold on the network. An electronic lock on the bottle cap and a radio-frequency tracking chip, and even lost pills can be located, minimizing opportunities for abuse.

And once you've reached that point, there's no reason to focus on the transactions in themselves. Blockchain tags have already been deployed to lock down merchandise in retail stores, with the sensors turning off if and when the tag registers legal sale. That same functionality can help freight companies protect inventory on the road, tying existing radio tagging systems into the network with an additional level of unbreakable security.

Every organization that stocks valuable physical products is going to want this capability. Overstock.com is farthest ahead and is now in position to start sharing its technology. Cognizant Technology Solutions has embraced consulting expertise to help management transform their processes in order to make it happen. If you're betting on the future of the way we buy and sell things (not to mention maintain a reliable inventory), these are the stocks I'd start with.

Wherever money moves, it will increasingly be digital, whether that's in a "crypto" blockchain-encrypted environment or via conventional, heavy-security credit and debit transfer networks. The payment stocks often lead Wall Street for a reason. PayPal, Square, and their counterparts haven't faltered despite fierce competition from Apple, Amazon, and everyone else who wants to horn in on their market. It's making them stronger.

These companies are still innovating their way toward a global, cash-free society, a revenue opportunity vast enough to support a lot of strong players and satisfy their shareholders. Start with the size of the opportunity and its rate of growth. While the number of transactions that payment companies can theoretically capture is a function of global GDP (rising about 3 percent a year), the role of cash is shrinking. As it is, there's $2 trillion in revenue for electronic payment companies to split, and that pool expanded seven times as fast as the global economy.

That's why I'm bullish on a lot of the payment stocks despite the perception that it's a crowded space. With overall revenue projected up a conservative 9 percent a year for the foreseeable future, everyone with a viable platform and business plan will have an additional trillion dollars a year of space to go around by 2022.

These companies are capturing more than their share of that space and then figuring out how to squeeze additional money out of it. PayPal is a great example. It's already a fixture of the online payment universe, running $600 billion a year across its network and generating $16 billion in transaction fees.

The sweet spot here is the company's mobile platform Venmo, which has become the default cash transfer system among Millennials who'd rather bump phones than turn on a desktop computer and load a site. Venmo is small right now at $70 billion a year in transaction volume but it's growing 80 percent a year, and it's a walled garden. It charges 3 percent of every transaction and another 1 percent to withdraw the money. Old-school banks and credit card issuers would cheer to get that kind of fee structure, but Venmo users pay it eagerly because they love the convenience.

(They even use it as a verb, like Google. They don't send each other an electronic payment. They "Venmo" each other. That's a great sign of loyalty to the platform.)

And that's where the sizzle is. Those fees are on top of what network partners charge to move the money onto the app in the first place. Companies can compete over who gets the highest-margin slice, but there's truly an incentive here for everyone to cooperate and make money together. That's always been the PayPal strategy, building on top of Visa and other card networks instead of spending billions to reinvent their wheel. It's why I can love Visa as well PayPal: the digital future is big enough for both companies.

But the next generation is where the growth is. We see 20 percent revenue growth a year ahead for PayPal and widening margins as new services like Venmo mature. Square is a similar story, bringing the credit card networks to previously untapped commercial settings in exchange for an added fee. Small merchants love the hardware and the service.

A few no longer even take cash. As their numbers rise, odds are good that more and more will accept bitcoin or other cryptocurrencies as well. Square has also been building out its cryptocurrency team, as CEO Jack Dorsey continues to focus on this evolving marketplace. In late 2018, Square actually surpassed Coinbase as the most-used Bitcoin trading platform. One way or another, that's the future.

And I wouldn't rule out Apple yet with its Apple Pay and now physical Apple Card systems. Apple Pay was good enough, turning the ever-popular phone into a credit card that you never had to take out of your pocket. The Apple Card reverses that appeal by acting as a tangible symbol of the Apple Pay account. Where it's revolutionary is that it solves credit card theft, theoretically eliminating conventional magnetic swipe or PIN verification entirely. The card is useless in itself if lost or stolen. The real brains are stored on your phone, where you'll be able to monitor spending and shut the physical card down if necessary.

In the meantime, the system exists to drive more retail activity into the Apple Pay network, where the company is already routing 20 million transactions a day, and volume is doubling year over year. For anyone else, that would be a huge win.

Unintended Consequences

One interesting detail here: the security aspect of blockchain transcends objects. At its core, the programming architecture this technology represents is often compared to a ledger where transactions are logged and monitored.

That includes financial transactions, which means that automatic blockchain systems are poised to replace huge swathes of the financial services back office—everything from stock transfer agency and custody to trade clearing and even proxy vote tracking. Trade settlement and account reconciliation are going to become trivial, even unconscious functions. The institutions that bear the burden today will reap enormous efficiencies if and when they invest in systems that make it happen.

Consider the fate of the lawyers. Most law firms bill a lot of hours for drafting documents and letters, which require time and professional skill. But this is an area where a bespoke contract can populate its own boilerplate fields, and a blockchain component will take over from there. DIY law services can use document assembly systems and chatbot advisers to offer cheap and reliable legal services, particularly for extremely common forms of legal dispute such as appealing a parking fine. Human lawyers are likely to remain the go-to for complex cases, but for simple matters, competent legal assistance will no longer be out of anyone's reach.

And imagine a blockchain-bound financial "advisor" that understands your saving, spending, and investment habits the moment you consent to share your information with it. Straight away, it's giving you bespoke advice that's not only informed by petabytes of fresh data from the market, but also by your own individual habits and needs. Insurance policies, likewise, can be exactingly tailored to meet your personal requirements. Expect a rapid decline in the profitability of insurers who live and die on off-the-shelf policies.

Not all robots moving through the future financial sector will run on blockchain, although the odds are good that many of today's "robot advisors" will operate on a similar protocol.

Most robo-managed accounts on the market today boil down to very simple allocations from a very limited shelf of pre-built portfolios. It's really nothing that someone could do on their own. That's okay because the goal is very different from hands-on investing. Investing is all about putting money to work to maximize risk-adjusted returns. What the robots are doing is gathering small pools of money from households that aren't investing now, the so-called "mass affluent" households. They're eliciting cash off the sidelines at a scale that previously wasn't really possible when dealing with conventional money managers. On that level, it's good for money flow because it sweeps these little pockets of cash and pours them into the market. As these products expand, they'll provide incremental support for the market as a whole, just as the dawn of retail mutual funds helped to feed middle-class money into Wall Street. So that's a good thing in general.

Do alert investors want in? Probably not. Confidentially and just between us, conventional money managers never had time for these accounts because there was no way to handle these amounts of cash profitably—the overhead ate up all the management fees. Robot advising makes it possible to provide something like professional service by automating the overhead out of the calculations and handling everything in volume. It's a volume form of investing, a mass market product. It's okay if you needed a solution, but higher-level investors who know their way around the market will find it a step down.

Now the first thing the human offers is different forms of scale and flexibility. Hilary Kramer, for example, can pursue more nimble and responsive strategies than a typical robot because I operate in more exclusive corners of the market. We don't need every trade to be tailored to fit a massive $10 billion pool of capital or a quarter-to-quarter investment policy statement. We can get a little smaller and a little more obscure, trading fleeting profit situations that would open and close before the robot platforms could even identify the opportunity.

And unlike the robots, we can be contrarian when it suits us, trading against the index. That's the definition of alpha, which is how well a portfolio can outperform the market as a whole by making active decisions to underweight some names while concentrating on others. Index funds, and the robots they support, are still obligated to maintain market weight on all these stocks, buying Exxon, for example, even though that company will probably remain dead money for months to come.

Every robot is only as good as the human expertise it's been programmed to emulate. The last problem here is that the programming so far can only mirror a random walk on the index funds. There isn't a long track record of data at this level to support real, human-powered investing. Until that happens, the humans who have seen it all won't be fooled by market situations that surprise the robots. And "flash crash" type events will happen. I know an investor who almost lost thousands of dollars because the brokerage firm's systems were confused by a simple stock split. The broker made it right when he complained, but the robots would have just kept humming along.

The Bottom Line for Early Adopters

Love or hate the bitcoin buzz, money is no longer in the hands of governments and the institutions they license. Investors looking to stay relevant and rich in the brave new world ahead can't afford to ignore blockchain's impact.

"Coins" will come and go. Like physical money, each one is just a symbol of a reservoir of value backed by something that matters to the owner. It's a token. What makes it meaningful is the way that the value and the token are fused together, becoming practically impossible to separate. That fusion process is the blockchain. And with so many people "mining" for crypto coins lately, you know I'll go with the hammer and shovel angle every time.

CHAPTER EIGHT

UNLEASHED:
PETS AND PROFIT

O ur relationship to the natural world has driven technology for thousands of years. Egyptians invented the first leash, as confirmed by a 4,000-year-old wall painting depicting a man walking his dog on one. Unlike pet mummification, this particular ancient Egyptian invention has truly caught on.

As our everyday lives recede from nature, we increasingly fill our artificial spaces with pets and their accoutrements. According to the American Pet Products Association (APPA) nearly 70 percent of U.S. households have pets, up significantly from 56 percent as recently as 1988. Further research by APPA shows that more households have pets than children, with 84.6 million households made up of adults and their beloved animals, and only 35 million households featuring adults and their (presumably equally beloved) children. APPA theorizes that the growth in pet households is tied to both Boomers and Millennials, the two most populous generations in the U.S., bringing home more and more furry friends.

What will this boom in pets mean for pet lovers in 2020 and beyond? Good news: the future holds many delights, from apps and eco-friendly pet wares, to cloning and robots.

The Internet of Pets

If you own a fitness tracker or have a social media account, rest easy. Your pet can have them too. A few examples of accessories of modern life tailored to our furry friends include:

- Clever Pet, an educational, interactive dog feeder
- Petbot, which records a video "selfie" of the pet when it approaches the device and emails it to the owner
- Kittyo, an app that enables absent cat parents to remotely play laser with their pet while recording the poor feline's desperate attempts to catch and eat a dancing ball of light
- Playdate, a smart ball that lets you play with your dog when you're away from home.

While these digital products are essentially toys (the equivalent of "stupid pet tricks" for the Internet), their existence opens the door to more serious applications on the horizon. Companies like Voyce and FitBark are taking cues from the human fitness tracker industry (see Chapter Two) to produce dog collars that communicate data to veterinarians. Smart litterboxes perform a similar function for cats, analyzing behavior and reporting back to the vet.

And then there are the companies like Whistle which sell GPS trackers that alert pet owners whenever the animal leaves a designated area. These systems only work in combination with tracking implants, effectively making animals nodes in the Internet of Things. From here, digital ideas multiply fast. North Carolina State University researchers are working on a chest harness for dogs that will record and transmit detailed biometric data, while other researchers are compiling a dictionary of barks to improve communication with canines.

All this development revolves around a single economic reality: we love our animals enough to pay extra to make sure they're not only safe and healthy but entertained. And whenever there's demonstrated demand, private enterprise steps up to supply solutions. The tracking functions alone use processing power that would make previous generations of computer scientists envious. We can't think of anything we'd rather do with that bandwidth.

Plain old veterinary care was once the privilege of extremely expensive breeding livestock on which whole families depended for their livelihoods. Now the biggest advances, like the fitness trackers and screening devices I just mentioned, are being made on behalf of cats and dogs, whose economic function is, well, a little less immediate.

Meet the New Cat (Same as the Old Cat)

And even if your beloved pet finally hits the limit of modern veterinary science, the agricultural industry has already funded alternatives. Step aside, selective breeding, and make room for genetic engineering. Rather than taking generations and producing millions of (frequently unwanted) animals, gene editing for agricultural purposes mean selecting for particular traits and creating specialty animals in a fraction of the time.

While selective breeding is an ancient technique, specific genetic modification of animals dates back to at least 2003 with GloFish, which—thanks to genetic tinkering—are available in fluorescent colors. A decade ago, Korean scientists oversaw the birth of four beagles that glowed with their own fluorescent light. A paleontologist is currently working to reverse engineer Jurassic-era chickens complete with dinosaur attributes like long tails, sharp teeth, and clawed fingers.

But what if you don't want a new type of pet, much less a prehistoric one? Now you can simply have the same pet, over and over again. Science has come a long way since Dolly the sheep, and Sooam, a leading South Korean pet cloning company, has already scaled up to the point where it costs just $50,000 to replicate a dog from a skin sample.

Rival companies like ViaGen, which cloned Barbra Streisand's dog, have already emerged, while PerPETuate offers a starter service that collects and preserves your precious pet's cells for just over $1,000, pending future improvements in the technology.

Other pets of the future will not even be animals. For fifteen years, Sony's now-defunct AIBO robotic pet dog was the most significant robotic pet since the Tamagotchi. While the company stopped producing replacement parts back in 2014, leading to robotic dog funerals and bereaved robotic pet parents, the studies produced during AIBO's brief stint on this planet bode well for future robotic "animal" companions once technology allows for greater authenticity.

That said, the AIBO was already quite an accomplishment, able to hear, see, and react with a programmed personality. Creating the full pet experience, however, complete with social intelligence and unconditional love, may take a little more work.

Despite AIBO's limitations, people reacted to and interacted with it like it was a real dog. Studies done showed that 80 percent of children found the companionship of the robotic dog comforting when they felt sad. In another smaller study, autistic children showed greater engagement with the robotic dog than with a non-robotic toy dog.

Another robotic pet, the Paro seal, produced remarkable results when used in a senior therapy setting. According to a 2016 study, dementia patients were given a Paro robotic seal for twenty minutes, three times a week in addition to standard care. As contrasted with a control group, the Paro seal patients showed decreased stress as demonstrated by lower pulse rates and higher oxygen levels, and decreased anxiety and depression, all of which contributed to a significantly decreased need for medication.

Bowl Game Champions

Disruption of the pet food industry has already begun—look no further than the eco-conscious, holistically wholesome, and organic products filling Fido's bowl for evidence. This trend toward healthier pet food, together with advancements in non-meat food like Beyond Burgers, suggest that the next leap in pet food will be away from animal protein entirely. This will be an amazing thing for the environment, as well as for producers of non-traditional pet food.

A 2015 study on global warming revealed that our cats and dogs produce sixty-four million tons of greenhouse gases per year, solely because of the amount of meat they consume. Meat production is a huge contributor to climate change. A 2017 study from a researcher at UCLA estimated that the 163 million cats and dogs in the U.S. consumed as much meat as 63 million people.

Several new and developing companies have taken on the challenge of greening up our pets' diets through insect power. EatSmall is working on dog food derived from fly larvae protein—one serving of their dog food is responsible for only one gram of greenhouse gases while an equal serving of beef-based food releases an astronomical 1,000 kilos of carbon dioxide. Tenetrio uses mealworms to make puppy treats. The mealworms are remarkable because they also produce nearly zero carbon emissions and are entirely edible. Most importantly, 90 percent of test puppies approved of their new snacks.

Unsurprisingly, cats are more finicky in their diet than dogs. All felines are obligate carnivores, meaning they must eat meat to live. But Berkeley biotech startup Wild Earth is working on growing bio-reactor meat to create "mouse" treats for cats. They fully intend to be the Beyond Meat of the pet food industry; in fact, the company already sells a mushroom-based dog treat and is also exploring koji-based snacks.

Getting Disruption on Your Side

Pet investing is surprisingly hot stuff on Wall Street these days. Between veterinary hospital stocks like VCA, luxury pet food, animal drug developers, and next-generation retail phenomena like Chewy, a lot of fortunes have already been made in this space. It's just getting started.

After all, the pet care industry is thriving and stretches from food and medicine production to grooming and veterinary services. You'll find both online and brick-and-mortar vendors catering to pet owners anxious to provide top of the line products for their four-legged companions. Estimates for the global pet care industry are remarkable, with expected growth from $132 billion in 2016 to $203 billion by 2025. In the U.S. alone, this is a $75 billion space, segmented across food ($30 billion), supplies/OTC medicine ($16 billion), vet care ($18 billion), live animal purchases ($2 billion) and other services ($6 billion).

It's also proved recession-proof, having grown significantly every year since 2007, including during the recession. According to a 2017–2018 survey of U.S. pet owners by the North American Pet Health Insurance Association, 80 percent of owners care for their pets like children, almost as many believe that their pets should receive food in quality that matches their own. Over 40 percent have purchased pet clothing or accessories and buy non-essentials such as toys on impulse.

When looking for a sense of who modern "pet parents" are, think young and old. Seniors and Millennials have the most pets. That's a sweet spot for our sense of the demographic center of gravity. (See Chapters One and Twelve.) Look for things that appeal to those ends of the population. While Baby Boomers account for 32 percent of pets owned, households headed by younger cohorts account for 62 percent of pet ownership.

The operative words are ease and specialization. Generic brick-and-mortar chains selling bulk commodity products are out. Convenience and value-added luxury are in. The people who are spending in this category love to spoil their babies and will pay exorbitant amounts for specialty care, grooming, and, yes, entire video game and TV systems for their beloved animals.

PetSmart is great, but it won't yield the rewards an emerging brand might. Look into smaller companies and start-ups doing unique things. Look globally. There is great work happening in Europe on insect-based pet food and in Asia on robotic and genetic advances.

From there, be practical, and don't be afraid to get messy. Unless you're looking seriously at robots, follow the money and daily necessities.

There's a limit to pet consumers' appetite for pet-geared technology. Pets aren't people. Animals may be entertained by an app, but tech doesn't have the totallizing grip on animals that it seems to have on humans. Animal needs are substantially physical: food, toys, waste management. A future where dogs and cats surf the net for hours is certainly possible, but you'll probably find that a steady stream of milk-bones and a game of catch will also do the trick.

So, while high-end technological innovations are eye-catching, the less glamorous parts of pet life will provide more reliable investment opportunities. Look for companies interested in revolutionizing the most basic elements of animal care. People are doing amazing things with dog waste bags, and there's always a new brand of cat litter.

In any event, this investment theme is so popular that ProShares has launched a Pet Care exchange-traded fund holding $28 million in shares of various pet-related companies: high-end food packager FreshPet, veterinary diagnostics maker IDEXX, Chewy.com, PetMed Express, all of the various animal drug developers, and so on. Look it up under the ticker symbol PAWZ. A similar fund from Gabelli, PETZX, weights its holdings slightly differently. Just take a look at either portfolio and start checking off the names you like.

I'm buying Chewy. It's an amazing company. The dot-com pet shipping failures moved first, and now this younger company is proving that the model really can work. Revenue soared from $200 million in 2014 to $3.5 billion now. That's a huge top-line ramp, which is what Wall Street covets more than anything else. Almost profitable even with that expansion rate, the company can basically make money whenever management decides to stop chasing growth and start cutting costs.

Over the years we've made a lot of money on veterinary medicine, but on a more prosaic level I couldn't help but notice recently that "GPS dog collar" was the top consumer product search online recently. A lot of ultra-small start-up vendors have established themselves as early players in that apparently hot category, but only Garmin is publicly traded. Tracking animals could be a nice boost for the company's bottom line.

If so, it'll be a perfect example of trends we track—the kind that turn into money for investors with their eyes on the prize.

We love our pets, and the furry side of the family was probably one of the few areas of the American budget where there was room for spending to increase significantly. Pet food has improved from scraps to kibble to butcher quality, refrigerated raw meat. I was just talking to someone from Los Angeles about filet mignon dinners for dogs at fifty dollars a plate! That's a little rarefied even by upscale standards, but it shows how high "mainstream" pet spending can go before it starts straining the stratosphere.

All in all, we spend double on healthcare per pet as we did a decade ago. PetMed specializes in the easy side of the business by selling veterinary medicine by mail. This isn't the bulk food business that drove the PetSmart revolution decades ago: there aren't any massive 100-pound bags shipped around the country, and unlike human pharmacy, regulatory constraints aren't a headache. We're looking at lean, mean envelopes and a cozy dot-com profit margin.

FreshPet has disrupted the high-end pet food business by selling all-fresh dog meals in grocery refrigerated aisles and is now testing slightly more traditional packaging as it hunts the mass market. Initial sales of the new product are already boosting revenue, which is ramping up at a rate of 30 to 35 percent per year. Wall Street is eyeing it as the kind of company that gets taken out before it even starts achieving its market potential, so build a position while you can. (See also: Blue Buffalo, which General Mills paid $8 billion to buy in 2018.)

Unintended Consequences

The past decade has seen huge positive trends in shelter and rescue work. Improvements in management, ethics, and technology have resulted in a significant decrease in shelter deaths by euthanasia or disease, while increasing adoption rates help clear out shelters in populated areas. Improved trap-neuter-return programs have also decreased animal overpopulation.

The 1970s saw one hundred cats and dogs euthanized per thousand humans in the population. In 2018, according to the ASPCA, that number is down to five cats and dogs euthanized per thousand humans, less than one tenth of the historical number. A coalition entitled Best Friends has set the goal of ending euthanasia in shelters by 2025.

Along with decreased euthanasia, the rescue world has seen a huge push towards "adopt don't shop" since the 1970s, and it's working. In the 1970s, 10 percent of pets were acquired from shelters, with a huge trend towards purebred cats and dogs, meaning that most were bought from breeders. Today, the number of shelter pets has increased to 35 percent, and the pressure of popular campaigns will drive that number higher in the next few years.

Will the trend of shelter adoptions be negated by bereaved owners cloning the same pet over and over again and no longer adopting new animals? Or, more likely, will the availability of cloning simply present another possible choice? As mentioned, trap-neuter-release and low-cost spay/neuter programs are effectively decreasing the number of feral animals waiting to be rescued. Already, shelters in high-demand areas partner with high-production, rural shelters overflowing with animals. As birthrates of unwanted animals continue to decline, there may be a shortage of adoptable animals that will be balanced out by cloning.

Breeding as a business model will weaken. Breeders could improve their public image if they partnered with rescues and shelters like major pet companies have, to push both rescue and bred animals. The adopt-don't-shop and No Kill shelter movements are going strong, and pet breeders have a well-earned, terrible reputation. Similarly, grim, old style shelters are making way for new facilities with kitten nurseries, on-site vet care, and integrated boarding kennels for already adopted animals.

Low-end pet food producers will also suffer. While there will always be a market for inexpensive pet food, it's not on a growth trajectory, and its market share will be chipped away by swankier, natural, even insect-based snacks.

Stationary pet services will lose business to mobile, in-home, on-demand, customized services—including grooming, vets, and end-of-life care. This will also include personalized, in-home training and care, rather than out-of-home training and boarding. Whole service industries already exist to take care of household animals. "Dog whisperers" and their cat-sensitive equivalents will be extremely popular and well compensated.

Delivery services and direct-to-consumer products will eat into pet store market share for everything from toys to treats to food and waste management. This will include specialized meal service and subscription box deliveries for animals as well as the more standard delivery of every-day essentials. Between consolidation and online competition, the local pet shop's days may well be numbered.

The Bottom Line for Early Adopters

More and more pet owners consider their pets a part of the family and treat them as such. Pets receive medical care, grooming, socialization, stimulation, and affection on par with human children, and some-times surpassing it.

Imagine a day in the life of your 2050 fur babies (a cloned dog named Fido the Fifth, a rescue cat, a genetically spawned dinosaur chicken, and a robot). Your pets get breakfast automatically downstairs while the smart house closes the bedroom door so they can't disturb mom and dad. They play video games and watch Dog & Cat TV. The remote is controlled through console interface that lets them change the channel with their paws/nose/beak.

And that's just before lunch. With all the technological advancements on the horizon combined with trends towards improved, humane care, the future is bright for pets and those that love them. They also provide a smart investment opportunity. Keep in mind that the future you invest in is the one you create. This is a terrific place to let your heart and desire to save the world—or at least a few cats and dogs—guide your investment. Put your money where you want the world to go, whether that means more sustainable pet food or the chance to actually have a conversation with your dog.

CHAPTER NINE

GIGS TO GIGAS:
THE SHARING ECONOMY AND YOU

A lot of the hard lines that once structured American life got blurry in the Great Recession of 2008–9, and under the combined weight of technology and capital some are melting down entirely. This is not necessarily a bad thing. In a lot of ways, we see the world more clearly when we roll back a few assumptions about the way we work, the way we support each other within the community, and the way we play.

Start with the way we work. Employment is a timeless institution. We work to live. We earn our bread and our place under the sky. Entrepreneurs start businesses and then hire help as needed to turn a profit. In the past, that much was obvious. But as the years passed, the market changed. For a few generations, a lot of us labored under the illusion that a career was something you did for forty hours a week, fifty weeks a year, from the day you graduated school to the day you retired on your sixty-fifth birthday. You had one boss, reported to work in one location alongside other people, and you received income from one source.

That was the model perpetuated in the 1950s when corporations like IBM wanted to lure professionals out of the cities into new suburban corporate campuses. It was wildly successful, spreading the dream of cradle-to-grave employment into Asia and elsewhere. But as with even the best dreams, we eventually needed to wake up. There's no covenant binding people to corporations, or corporations to people. Corporations come and go. Their HR needs change. Our needs change too.

Even in the 1950s, employment tenure was lower than many of us believe. Most young adults changed jobs every two to three years, spending roughly the same time in each position as they do now. Americans across all age groups tended to leave a company and move on at least twice a decade. They were all ultimately free agents. It's just that that freedom is more obvious now, when 16 million of us work for ourselves rather than a company (unless we're independent contractors).

In Uber's World, Hustle Is Power

This is the gig economy. With the rise of the Internet, white-collar professionals are no longer bound by location. Some work remotely where the cost of living is low, accepting standard U.S. pay while paying overseas rents. Others have even become full-fledged "digital nomads," touring the world with no fixed address and occasionally checking in with the home office when they need to collaborate on a long-term project.

Of course these people are often high-powered IT and media professionals who can transmit their expertise from another continent as effectively as from the cubicle over. That's the dream. Most workers in the "gig economy" don't have that luxury. They're hustling to make ends meet, never quite amassing the bankroll to move to Australia. They're needed on site. A full 4 million of them are Uber drivers. They're free agents who work for the company's app, driving where the app tells them to go and accepting the money the app gives them.

Labor is everywhere. Even when someone has a full-time job, most of us are willing to trade those few hours here or there to make a little extra money. It can be a hard life, but the ambition and the aspiration are commendable. In a lot of ways, it's a more intimate version of the entire Silicon Valley power career. You take a risk and open your free time up to the "app" or the entrepreneurial life. Maybe you build something.

It beats staying home and watching TV all day. Maybe tomorrow you'll find another gig or simply turn off the app. In the meantime, the people around you actually get where they need to go.

Freelancers Helping Freelancers

We see this improvisational ethic at work from a managerial perspective as well. As more employees become free agents themselves, institutional barriers separating them from the boss come down. Suddenly they aren't in a hierarchical relationship anymore. They're simply two people brought together out of a shared interest in exchanging a little time for money: one side of the transaction receives the time and the right to dictate the parameters for how it's used, while the other puts forth the effort and receives the money. A few weeks or months later, the roles may easily reverse, turning the former boss into the employee and the employee into an entrepreneur.

Anyone can start a business now and give it a portion of their time. You don't have to give it sixty hours a week. You don't even have to give it ten hours a week. You've probably seen the "Four-Hour Work Week" ads. They resonate with people because the message is attractive and true. Nobody needs to work longer hours—or work harder in the time they commit to working. All we have to do is allocate our time more effectively: do the smartest and most necessary work in the hours we have and cooperate with other people to share the heavy lifting as well as the rewards.

That's how Uber works, after all. You own your car just like you own your time. You volunteer a little of that ownership to someone who needs that car or a few hours of that time. In exchange, you receive money. The car would have been sitting there in the garage. You might've been sitting in the house enjoying yourself. Neither of you were generating any wealth for anyone. Get off the sofa, hit the road, and the money will start coming in. Uber makes it easier to connect with the customer, and in return Uber takes a slice of the revenue.

Someone with a business idea, but lacking the skills to pull it off, can start a business online today by shelling out fifty dollars for access to freelance platforms. Then he can offer the people who do have the necessary skills a cut of the anticipated cash flow which his great idea will generate. And if it doesn't turn out to be such a great idea after all? They gambled a little and lost. Maybe the next idea will fare better. This is the blessing and curse of the gig economy: You get what you pay for. While a lot of free, or nearly free, talent is available somewhere in the world, it isn't always a smooth or professional experience.

But that idea man has become a venture capitalist. Having seeded a lot of these companies myself back in the last boom, the pattern plays out exactly the same way, only on a larger scale. People with money fund an idea or get matched up with someone with an idea but no money. They use the money to make the idea happen. Good ideas keep the money flowing, repaying the initial investment and setting the table for the next allocation for the next tempting idea. Fail, and you've wasted the money and the time.

Of course this lifestyle isn't for everyone. A lot of people loved being employees back in the 1950s, and I suspect quite a few are nostalgic for that era even if they never actually experienced it themselves. But more are hungry, ambitious, or both. Finding work isn't easy, and it's even more difficult for those who want to preserve their liberty.

In many ways, the gig economy is a return to an older style of work, before corporate managers saw the benefits of reducing turnover and cultivating the same pool of human capital for a generation or two. Back then, it was all networking, creating connections, making friends, and then making a mutually beneficial deal.

You can be a corporation of one and squeeze incremental bits of work out of anyone on the planet who has money and a need for the kind of work you can do. Your Uber territory, as it were, is boundless. All you need is an Internet connection and a little old-fashioned hustle. For those with few traditional prospects (lower-income households, lower education levels, rural areas), it's a godsend.

From One Gig to the Next

That's a miracle in itself because a lot of drivers are going to need to find new ways to support themselves and their families. Some will be cab drivers replaced by Uber and other car sharing networks. Some will be truck drivers whose routes have been automated. Ultimately the Uber drivers themselves will find themselves on the sharp end of competition when their own cars take over, rendering them obsolete.

"Driver" is the most prevalent job in most states for a very good reason. Freight is the backbone of the U.S. economy, and as we'll see in Chapter Ten, the freight lines are on the verge of mass automation, throwing millions of people out of work. The next decade or two will see dramatic shifts in the operation of roads, highways, and transportation systems. Travel and transport as a service, as seen with Uber and Lyft, have the potential to create new markets almost overnight.

These companies have made so much headway because no matter what you think about the stocks, they play a crucial role in the communities where they operate. When Uber started in Austin, Texas in 2014 (in the face of extreme local outcry), DWI arrests dropped by 16 percent in a year. Drunks had an affordable and easy alternative to taking their own cars home in a city without an entrenched, conventional taxi fleet. That was a true GameChanging moment.

Likewise, a 10 percent drop in DUI arrests was observed in Seattle in Uber's first year of operation there. Self-driving cars will be even safer, and cutting the driver out of the loop will probably lower the price of a ride by up to 25 percent, which can only create a virtuous cycle for the riders and the networks. The drivers, of course, need to think ahead because as we've seen, automation is coming to this space.

So too, then, must we consider how the job markets will be affected. Drivers may be made redundant, but how soon? Taxi drivers and truck drivers might not be driving their old routes in person, but from remote control hubs as a backup. Technicians and maintenance workers will surely be needed to service these vehicles. Those who've allowed their negotiation skills and hustle to atrophy in a relatively secure nine-to-five relationship will need a lot more adjustment and maybe some concentrated retraining. (There's going to be a big market for that and big money for the people who can serve as coaches.)

The drivers who've already been hustling are more likely to land on their feet after they're ejected from the driver's seat. As independent contractors, they recognize the value of their time and how much work they need to do in order to pay the bills. New kinds of companies will probably emerge to help them finance autonomous cars of their own and get them on the road, either individually or as a consortium. After all, the first few years of transition will require backup drivers to take the wheel in an emergency. They'll see the writing on the wall then. The smart ones will come up with a plan.

Either way, the next decade or two will see dramatic shifts in the operation of roads, highways, and transportation systems. Travel and transport as a service, as seen with Uber and Lyft, can create a new market overnight.

Meanwhile, there is already a distinct trend among young urbanites and even suburbanites like my daughter to prefer ride sharing and app-booked driving services to individual car ownership. The day of the family car in every garage is fading like the horse and buggy did before. The youth of tomorrow will look at transportation as a shared resource: pay and be the boss or owner for a few miles or invest in the car as a career resource.

It turns out that ride sharing was very much a feature of society in the days of the Victorian Hansom cab. Charles Dickens's letters show him to have been a prolific cab-sharer, likely for social as much as economic reasons. When going out with a friend he often asked them to pick him up from home in a cab which they would share on the way to their destination.

There is also a tremendous opportunity for autonomous vehicle owners to use their cars for a side-hustle: rather than parking for the duration of an eight-hour workday, the car could be earning its owner money by taking passengers around in a ridesharing plan.

The Shared Economy

An Uber driver owns his car or leases it from the company. An Airbnb landlord owns or rents an apartment or house and rents it out to people looking for shelter outside the conventional hotel experience. In both cases, the company facilitates the transaction but does none of the on-site work, hires none of the people as employees, and rarely owns any of the assets.

These are not taxi and hotel companies, nor even taxi and hotel replacements. That would only be as accurate as saying the modern Amazon is "an online bookstore" when its real business revolves around leveraging massive computing power in order to support Prime subscriptions and a burgeoning universe of third-party merchants. What Uber and Airbnb really do is structure and monetize the transition from the old suburban universe of one household, one job, one car, one house into a world where the definitions are more flexible and more transactional.

Have a job but no car? Hire someone else to take you to work. Have a car but no job? The car is your job. Have a job but no house? Rent a room from someone. Have a car and no house? The day is coming when you'll be able to work out direct transportation-for-lodging deals on a website somewhere. Of course people have been doing that face to face for generations.

And the roles shift with circumstances. Got another car? Rent it to a driver and it makes you money while you drive. Too many people want to stay at your house? It's time to think about expanding. Have a job already but simply want more money? Take a little leisure time and rent out a resource. Share what you have. The apps determine how you're compensated, but you can always find your own counterparties and negotiate on your own.

The Reality Show that Never Ends

Sometimes it seems like the biggest advances can only be recognized in the long-term rear view, while day to day the pace of innovation feels incremental at best. With Wall Street weighing the odds of a 5 to 10 percent camera enhancement on the latest generation of iPhone as a do-or-die decision, we need to look back a few decades to really see how much 24/7 wireless web and email have transformed our lives.

It's also a moment of glory for the networks. CBS is turning into a leader in going direct across the Internet to its audience—the company's streaming-only channel could be a real GameChanger when the historians sum up this era years from now. At that time, I'm betting we'll be looking backward with them and counting our profit.

So leave Netflix to drift until it breaks out of its trading band, whichever comes first. The rest is short-term noise obscuring what's still a solid, long-term disruption story. I love the innovation that this company has already unleashed. In barely a decade the pivot from DVD mail-in rental to independent, streaming-only film studio has been profound. The business model remains unchanged, however. The goal here isn't replacing Hollywood. It's redefining premium television for a future beyond the legacy cable TV box.

Netflix has managed to coexist for its entire lifetime with HBO, for example. They're both premium channels, charging millions of people a few dollars a month for access to a mix of proprietary content and licensed shows. People who love television subscribe to both. If money gets tight, they can always pull the cable cord and suddenly they have (on average) $100 a month to work with.

After all, while you can only watch one show at a time, we all appreciate variety. As the cable stranglehold weakens, I suspect the future will leave most households with three to five premium subscriptions replacing the old video bundle. There's a lot of talk about Disney as one of those subscriptions. That's great. Disney is cartoons, superheroes, Star Wars, and family fare. I doubt it will compete directly for the HBO crowd, much less people who love Netflix originals.

The Disney Channel has lived on the cable box for decades without killing HBO. I think Netflix with its 149 million users will coexist just fine here. That said, the hype around Disney Streaming has gotten out of hand as well. They're paying a fortune buying other media franchises and developing new ones as well, but unlike Netflix, they're struggling to grow. Going direct to consumers will help the margins but doesn't trigger a dramatic reappraisal of the entire company.

Here's the thing: all of these companies are desperate for content. They want to take a chance on the next viral sensation. The professional studios are packaging every show they can think of, and still the streaming channels crave more. YouTube is always hungry for video, and anyone with a phone can record streaming-quality video and publish it on the site. Go viral there, and you're a star.

All modern children know this, almost intuitively. The rest of us could benefit from letting it sink in. The barriers to entry have fallen. Everyone can be a media figure and be on something like TV. There's no arcane studio system, no hurdles you need to leap before you get an audition. All the gatekeepers are irrelevant now. Write a song. Paint a picture. Take a photo. Produce a home movie, talk show, or animated epic. Suddenly you're a content producer, monetizing what would otherwise have been a hobby that distracted you from your job.

For the minutes you spend on that project, your hobby becomes your gig. Again, our kids already know this. People just like them and their friends have become online celebrities, stars of their own reality shows. Like all those stars, success is not about who you know. It's about who the camera reveals you to be.

Getting Disruption on Your Side

The most obvious thing to invest in here is yourself. Even if you're working for someone in a job you love, think like an entrepreneur. Kickstart a side hustle. It doesn't need to be extremely lucrative unless you need it to be.

Maybe you dye yarn for knitters. Sell it on Etsy, which exists to structure the transition between factory-scale consumption relationships and artisanal production. Maybe you find old trash that only collectors would want, but you know what it's worth. Sell it on eBay. Both of these sites blur the barrier between my stuff and yours, someone who buys and someone who sells. You're taking the first steps into the mercantile world, becoming a small-scale storekeeper or factory owner. It doesn't need to take up all your time. It doesn't need to pay all your bills. You're sharing your week, and your customers are sharing their money.

You have a side hustle. And for some of us, the side hustle becomes a career and a life. We're free agents. Business ebbs and flows, we have great seasons and lean ones, but we'll never get laid off. We may never even retire if we like what we're doing. Not coincidentally, that also describes a professional investor's life, and that's what I wish for you some day. How old are Warren Buffett and Carl Icahn again? If they hated their hustle, they would have quit decades ago.

And as for which stocks I would buy to monetize this transition for myself, I'd focus on companies that own the underlying assets as well as the innovators whose technology puts that inventory to work. Uber and Lyft waited too long and accepted too much venture capital before we could get a taste. They were overvalued from the start. Airbnb faces the same ominous math.

So buy into the people who make other pieces of the gig economy happen. Buy social media. Twitter is where anyone can become famous on the Internet for five minutes. It's where CEOs can communicate directly and instantaneously with customers, shareholders, and competitors, bypassing the old PR system that kept us apart. And it's where we can talk back. Even the president is communicating in real time with zero institutional filter.

The family phone is how your kids become Instagram celebrities who make money being teens in public. You need an updated phone to be an Uber driver. You need good broadband to attract Airbnb guests to your home. If you've got the hustle, technology helps you monetize. YouTube runs the kids' videos, and Facebook owns Instagram.

And if you're looking for the disruptive startups of tomorrow to pay you rent, WeWork is not public yet, but once again, this could be the hot stock of tomorrow. The company was founded in 2010 by Adam Neumann to help startups and small companies use shared workspaces to bring down the cost of private office spaces in large, expensive cities. WeWork negotiates long-term contracts with the buildings, and then re-rents portions of the space on a shorter-term basis.

As more and more startups look for a more professional office space than the garage, WeWork is providing that "mezzanine infrastructure." The company is currently valued at $16 billion and is continuing to provide competition towards traditional leasing agencies such as Boston Properties.

Unintended Consequences

Go back to Planet Uber for a moment. Beyond the technical programming, we must consider the changes to our society as a result. So much of our social lives and economy are tied to home location and vehicle ownership or ride services. For years, people living in cities may not have needed a car because of robust public mass transit systems. That experience will soon be arriving at Main Street, U.S.A. You can live anywhere and commute wherever you need to go.

That's incredibly liberating. And the ramifications run a lot deeper than just how you get from place to place. As the old work economy evaporates, life reverts to a series of transactions between people with resources and people with needs. We trade what we have for what we want. Nothing is handed to us, and nothing is assumed. For some people, that's horrifying. To them I say, if you want life to be stable and secure, make it that way. That's not what life was ever all about.

The Bottom Line for Early Adopters

If you've spent any time at all in the gig economy you know the rewards and the frustrations of being your own boss and leveraging your resources as you see fit. You will fail and probably have already failed numerous times. That's how we learn!

But in a world where other people's companies fail and throw tens of thousands of people out of work with surprising frequency, upsets are going to be inevitable either way. When modern workers change jobs every three to five years, it isn't always by choice. Most of the time, it's because the old job ended or became unbearable, or we found something better and jumped. Either way, with enough hustle, most of us can find a way to hold everything together until we're in a position to reach for better things.

The important thing is that you fail on your own terms because that's how you can enjoy the benefits of your success when it comes. Maybe you'll become a new kind of star. Maybe you'll become a new kind of tycoon. Maybe you'll spend as little time as possible working to pay the bills so you can relax on the beach. And more likely, your road will take you somewhere in between. As long as you realize that work and play are no longer all-or-nothing opposites, you can split your resources into fractions and allocate each fraction as you see fit.

After all, we do it all the time on Wall Street whenever we create a derivative instrument or take a company public. Take something that formerly belonged to one person, whether that's you or your current boss. Slice it up and share it out. Some pieces, you can sell to the highest bidder. Others, you can afford to give away.

CHAPTER TEN

Retail Therapy: Amazon and the Mall

From nomadic hunter-gatherers trading meat for skins and tools, to settlers trading produce at farmer's markets, to modern Big Box stores, and now the endless online marketplace, trade is the heart of civilization. Only the logistics have changed.

Raw materials and finished products can move around the world. Distance no longer matters. The world has flattened out, and now we can buy from anywhere and ship to anyone. In that world, convenience and price are the only essentials. Given the choice, we tend to want what we want *now*. And we don't want to pay too much.

I've just described a company called Amazon.

Taking Cues from the Universal Catalog

Remote consumption was already commonplace in the 40s and 50s when we would pick out clothes and toys from a catalog and they arrived a few weeks later, but the Internet changed everything. Marketplaces such as eBay, Amazon, and more recently AliBaba and AliExpress have become staples for shoppers as well as entrepreneurs worldwide.

The true leverage that companies such as Amazon have is the wide-reaching network of businesses, entrepreneurs, manufacturers, and logistics companies which come together into an intricate dance. The consumer orders an item and immediately the entire machine starts working to deliver the item as quickly and safely as possible. Regardless of where the item comes from—the U.S., Europe, China, or Africa—there are companies ready to move it in the right direction.

From warehouse to truck, from sorting to plane, from courier to your doorstep. The relationships aren't complicated on paper. But every one of those stops involves at least several people, timetables, and many potential failure points. In theory, this complexity would reward shorter routes and more localized relationships. But in practice, most of the things we buy today are can come from anywhere.

A lot of the time, that's still the mall across town or even right there in your neighborhood. We still love to see new things before we buy them. The catalog or web page is a decent substitute, but for a lot of people, it's always going to be a substitute. Then there are the rituals that bring us to traditional retail events like "Back to School" (as I write this the parking lots are filling up and cash registers are ringing) or the various holiday sales that punctuate an otherwise secularized calendar.

I'm not a big fan of Black Friday, but I get it. People don't even show up to shop. They just want to get caught up in the crush of the crowd. When they buy things, it's almost as a way to reward the mall for making the crowd possible. If they were thinking, they'd simply take pictures of the things they want to buy to remind them to search online later.

That's theoretically a problem for the retail stocks that collectively represent over $10 trillion in market capitalization worldwide, but the nuance is an important one for investors to understand. Retail chains ebb and flow depending on the experience they provide. It was never about the merchandise itself, though stocking the shelves the right way was a big part of that experience. The catalog retailers got very big in their day. Walmart, the ultimate brick-and-mortar competitor, put an end to that.

Classic retail required a storefront to warehouse merchandise close to the point of sale, as well as to provide shoppers with a place to browse the options available. Distance to the nearest store was critical, forcing retailers to build out their local footprint. This is extremely expensive, forcing even the strongest and most pervasive chains to invest heavily in their real estate plan in order to grow.

It has also created a lot of redundant support systems for each location. While distribution, marketing, and other corporate activities can be centralized, others like IT, in-store inventory, and customer service need to be duplicated across every store in the chain. Each store also needs to stock a reasonable level of merchandise, multiplying inventory costs. In light of these dynamics, it is no wonder that profit margins throughout the industry have hit a wall.

Smaller franchises reap more modest benefits of scale and are more vulnerable to shifting consumption trends. It's a little easier for larger retail networks, but size does not free a chain from the need to keep bolting largely redundant locations onto its operation. All retailers struggle to outflank competitors and keep leveraging their headquarters and warehousing costs across more points of sale.

Online merchants don't have these issues. From the earliest mail-order companies to Amazon, scale is more closely tied to efficiency because there are no stores to multiply. Distribution comes directly from a central warehouse that grows in line with shopper demand. The advantage is obvious.

The Showroom Effect

Despite the online-only model's fundamental advantage here, most store-based retail have survived the new wave of competitors because brick-and-mortar merchants know how to actively sell. Seeing merchandise on display gives shoppers a chance to discover new products and make impulse buys. Trained floor staff can also recommend products, boosting overall sales efficiency as well as moving inventory that management wants to get off the shelves.

Amazon won its initial battles by concentrating on product categories—books and then other media—that lend themselves to on-demand transactions. If you wanted a specific book or DVD, you would search for the title online, find it on Amazon, and place your order. Books are closed until you start leafing through the pages, and you'd better believe that the "take a look inside" feature was one of the first Amazon developed.

Clothing, home décor, hardware, and especially groceries have been a lot trickier to distribute on that kind of on-demand, search-ready basis. This has been a lifeline for stores that compete effectively in those markets, giving chains like Pier 1 the boost they need to survive where once-vibrant retail giants like Barnes & Noble have failed. So the brick-and-mortar merchants have held their own because their physical inventory and showrooms are better suited to the way we shop.

The Real Retail Landscape

People who spend all day in front of a screen sometimes forget what's going on in the real economy. Admittedly, electronic commerce remains the most dynamic slice of the retail universe, and an investor who wants pure exposure really only has four options.

You can go with Amazon, the giant that now dominates half of the online market and is still expanding its presence at a healthy 25 percent a year.

Online-focused contrarians can pursue niches with eBay or the much smaller Etsy, Wayfair, and Overstock.com. Between them, these stocks control maybe 9 percent of digital retail.

The third option is to skip the stores entirely and focus on the technology companies that build the online shopping carts and support the credit card transactions. That's PayPal and upstart Shopify.

Or you can go back to conventional brick-and-mortar or, more realistically, unified store-and-screen platforms that beckon every shopper offline and online wherever the urge strikes. When a retailer finds the keys to survival and success, it doesn't matter where the final sale gets booked or whether the merchandise is shipped or carried off in a shopping bag. Growth is growth. And when the chain is small and growing fast enough, shareholders can make dot-com levels of money.

Either way, the obvious choice isn't really a pure play on retail anymore. Amazon is increasingly focused on Cloud computing services, and even its commercial operations are directed less at selling its own inventory than creating a marketplace for entrepreneurial third parties to exploit.

A full 65 percent of all retail dollars on the Amazon platform and 85 percent of the company's growth came from these third parties last year. Direct sales are already a small piece of the overall footprint and growing smaller every day.

Meanwhile, conventional brick-and-mortar stores remain the center of the consumer universe, generating sixteen times as much economic activity as Amazon last year. Walmart still dominates that world but it doesn't even account for 10 percent of that admittedly fragmented landscape.

What's striking is that Amazon is so popular on Wall Street and so highly valued that it distorts the market's view of where retail dollars really go.

Amazon generates just as much profit as Walmart, which now has reached a phase where it takes a vast amount of growth to move the fundamental needle. As a result, WMT has barely 30 percent of the Wall Street footprint as its electronic archrival.

It doesn't have to make sense. Amazon simply rates a huge premium as the category-killing company that terrifies a lot of retail investors. Walmart, on the other hand, is seen as friendly and reliable, the status quo that disruptors are eager to divide and conquer. For me, however, even that battle of the giants misses the real story and the real opportunity in retail today. Amazon and Walmart combined are barely 15 percent of all U.S. retail.

There's easily $3 trillion a year left for everyone else to fight over. Even at miserable 2 percent margins, that's $60 billion a year in theoretical profit. Companies capturing part of that market from rivals will grow faster and deserve valuations closer to Amazon. The rest compare more closely to Walmart.

Wall Street doesn't see a lot of the winners. A lot of public retail stocks are the entrenched department store chains and mall outlets that are truly vulnerable to more nimble competitors.

Look at a Wall Street list, and you'd think all American consumers shop at Amazon, Home Depot, and Walmart exclusively, with a thin veneer of activity at Lowe's, Target, TJX, and Costco.

That's it. No other retail stock rates even 3 percent of the big consumer portfolios, which are weighted by market capitalization and not market share. As a result, dozens of day-to-day retailers in modern American life get ignored. And only two of the companies I just mentioned—Amazon and Costco—have sales increasing by 10 percent a year or more.

The entrenched retail giants simply aren't dynamic. And the truly dynamic chains are still too small to ping Wall Street's screens. It's no wonder the analysts look at the sector and simply see Amazon, already a giant and fast growing, while all the other major players stall, stagnate, or actively erode. (Remember Sears? JCPenney?)

Whenever you're looking at retail stocks, remember that Main Street needs to play the biggest role in your calculations. Follow the shoppers. Follow the money they spend. Wall Street can't see the emergent trends hidden in Amazon's shadow.

There are weak links in that food chain as well. The department stores are missing. The drugstores are missing. They're out of favor on Wall Street, so they just don't have the market heft to show up on the lists. Some people say they're doomed. After hearing that story for years, I'm less and less convinced. They may not be growing fast as a group, but they aren't giving up a lot of ground either. Amazon has to fight harder now.

Even the flashy electronic upstarts get ignored. Some are a lot more vibrant than Amazon at this stage in their business cycle. If you want the thrill of buying Amazon at twenty dollars back in 1997, this is the place to look. Buying Amazon here in the 2020s isn't a bad decision, but it won't wind the clock back a single day. The future is with today's dynamic sites and their offline counterparts.

Send More Drones (and Robot Trucks)

The future belongs to long-haul autonomous trucks travelling over great distances within the controlled landscape of superhighways. Solving the issue of how to drive the last mile will be another evolving trend. Trucks could arrive at a central location outside a city, where human-controlled delivery trucks (in person or remote-controlled) take the cargo to its final destination.

The more obvious evolutions will be in both the home and commercial delivery space and in moving people in a regular pattern. Many different designs for autonomous delivery drones are in the works and making deliveries right now, depending on what goods are involved. Small, slow, and steady, these durable and dependable robots will become a common sight in our downtowns and neighborhoods.

Even if private car ownership doesn't vanish, we're sure to see automated freight take over the highway, which will decimate the service industries which cater to truck drivers: truck stops, diners, motels, and more. Retail will continue to migrate away from face-to-face purchases as automated delivery systems become ubiquitous.

Autonomous delivery vans will be equipped with drones to handle the last few feet of the delivery process. With garages and driveways no longer required for cars, home-owners may have a dedicated delivery area. Traditional carriers such as Fedex, USPS, and UPS will go out of business as purveyors of driverless vans and aerial drones (mainly Amazon) take their market share completely.

The autonomous vehicles of the future are almost certainly going to be electric. The effect on the oil industry will be jarring. Approximately half of the world's oil production ends in gasoline. The demand for petrochemicals is large, but it pales in comparison to today's global thirst for gasoline. Hand in hand, the driverless future and the electric car will likely devastate Big Oil.

Automated freight is likely to be one of the earliest and biggest opportunities. Use of autonomous vehicles is set to save the U.S. haulage industry over a $100 billion a year. A Morgan Stanley estimate suggested automated freight delivery could save businesses $168 billion annually, combining contributions from reduced labor costs, saved fuel, fewer accidents, and increased utilization of equipment.

Amazon, Robby, Starship, Nuro, Marble, and Dispatch all support autonomous ground delivery drones. Sure, Amazon wants to send out a fleet of drone aircraft to deliver packages, but these ground vehicles are small and mighty. Experimental pilot programs are underway, with Marble delivering for Yelp, and Starship for DoorDash. Reports indicate that in the future, 80 percent of purchased items will be delivered by autonomous delivery pods or drones.

TuSimple, Embark, Ike, Kodiak Robotics, and Waymo are the names to watch in long-haul autonomous trucking. Despite 4 million professional drivers on the road today, we still need at least 50,000 more as older drivers retire without being replaced. (Apparently nobody wants to join a profession in danger of becoming extinct in our lifetime.) Autonomous trucks can solve part of that problem—current plans call for a driver to be available for at least part of the trip, whether that is on board the truck for last-mile navigating of city streets or at a remote-control station, or simply to check periodically the tires and oil.

Trains or "platoons" of linked autonomous trucks could be a normal sight on the nation's open highways. Several companies are vying now for a piece of the $700 billion trucking market and hoping to be the first with autonomous trucks. The more obvious evolutions will be in both the home and commercial delivery space and in moving people in a regular pattern. Many different designs for autonomous delivery drones are in the works and making deliveries right now, depending on what goods are involved. These durable and reliable robots will become a common sight in our downtowns and neighborhoods.

And that's just what's possible in the next few years. Beyond that, evolving autonomous technology will make its way into ships and trains, making these bulk container carriers that much more efficient. Cargo will travel seamlessly from its point of origin, to local ports and stations, be loaded onto self-driving trucks, and arrive on our doorsteps courtesy of delivery drones and pods—seamlessly automated through the supply chain.

With the autonomous vehicle comes a huge drop in the cost of transporting goods and people. Over long distances, there will be substantial time savings as well, with self-driven trucks requiring no breaks other than to refuel or for routine maintenance. Local delivery will also change, with autonomous vehicles delivering pizzas and packages to your door. Some of these will be self-driving road vehicles, but others may well be aerial drones like Amazon's famous Prime Air service, which made its first completely autonomous delivery in 2016. We can already project the social and safety benefits by looking at the effects of Uber—the relative low cost and the reliability of the current human-powered Uber service has significantly depressed DUI convictions.

One other area that will see immediate growth is long-haul trucking. Various companies are testing different technologies for autonomous trucks up to and including NHTSA Level 5 full control. Initial deployment will probably rely on "truck train" systems for highway driving, with connected trucks working together and last-mile remote control by a human driver at the home location.

So many of our consumer and commercial goods are transported by ship and by train, and those industries are also looking at autonomous controls. The autonomous ship market was estimated at $6 billion in 2018 and projected by 2030 to reach $13 billion. Increased reliance on sea trade, maritime safety regulations, and tourism are key factors working for the growth of this market. Despite a recent slump in the shipbuilding industry, countries in Europe, particularly Scandinavian countries such as Denmark and Norway, are heavily involved in developing autonomous sea vessels.

Rolls-Royce in the UK and Kongsberg Gruppen in Norway are two main players in this market, with contracted work involving autonomous sea vessels. Rolls-Royce is a leading manufacturer of ship engines and has expanded into other segments. It is a leader in new marine technology. Another leader in this field is Wartsila in Finland, a major developer of automated marine vessel systems. In late 2018 Wartsila finished testing a dock-to-dock system where an automated ferry visited three ports in Norway without interruption along the entire route.

Along with autonomous ship travel, public and political will is strong for autonomous train travel. Because of several recent commuter train accidents, calls have arisen for greater safety procedures and technology. These changes can be applied to freight trains as well. Demand for autonomous trains is on the rise around the world, as it's an efficient means of travel for the public and commercial goods as well. Cities in Europe and Asia are working with the industry to develop and deploy autonomous trains and underground subway mass transit systems. The autonomous train market is projected to climb to $200 billion by 2024.

Don't discount Volvo, Caterpillar, and John Deere as leaders in autonomous farm equipment, mining, and large industrial trucks. (Volvo is testing an autonomous trash truck.) These products are out there now and have been in the field already for several years, doing repetitive tasks in an open environment where there are few people or other vehicles around.

Don't think that all the benefits will be to city-dwellers and the companies which service them. Autonomous freight has the potential to completely change how we understand logistics. The Japanese logistics company Nippon Express is partnering with Volvo subsidiary UD Trucks to test highly automated vehicles on a 1.3 kilometer stretch of road between a sugar plant and a processing line. There are tricks being deployed to bring this technology to the marketplace as soon as possible—the Silicon Valley company Peloton has created trucks which automatically follow the truck in front.

A human driver remains in the loop, controlling the first vehicle, while the rest of the convoy follows automatically. 65 percent of U.S. consumable goods are brought to market by truck. It's estimated that fully autonomous freight would reduce operating costs by 45 percent, a saving between $85 billion and $124 billion. With freight costs making up a sizeable portion of the cost of goods, this could have a radical impact on the affordability of all manner of products, opening up huge new markets. This will dovetail neatly with improvements in how products are manufactured and stored. 3-D printers, automated factories, and robot-operated warehouses open up a future of seamless AI-optimized supply chains.

Most likely, small, urban-area delivery vehicles are poised to have the greatest immediate impact and growth. Multiple firms are working on the technology. There might not be one or two big winners here— several of the designs are specialized depending on the goods being delivered. Much of the current growth and future expansion is in shared autonomous ride vehicles and small, urban delivery pods like Renault's Ez-Pro or Toyota's e-Palette.

Be Your Own Retailer

The good news is, anyone can start an online 'dropshipping' business and make a profit by selling imported goods. It's been a long time coming, but importers are no longer bound by their own logistics. Shipping a parcel from China rarely costs more than $150. And if you sell at a 50 percent margin (which is still much cheaper than buying similar items in a brick-and-mortar store), you only need to buy about $200 worth of product to make a nice $100 profit.

This has become the go-to answer to the frequently asked question, "How do I make money online?"

And for good reason—almost anyone can register a business and start selling items they choose by the next day. Then they buy the items with the money and deliver within the time-period they specify. Some companies always want to deliver, so they tell customers that delivery takes as long as a month!

For most consumers, that's a long wait—and not always worth the better prices. But even a small minority of buyers can make this profitable and desirable as a business model.

But this brings us to bad news. Given that a lot of Chinese manufacturers produce knock-offs, frequently re-using products they had previously been legally contracted to manufacture, they get stopped by customs.

After all, they're still producing their client's product, just under their own label. This makes it a viable product—which is legal in China, where copyright and trademark law don't really exist, but in the U.S., it gets people's things taken by the government.

Companies in IT, with Apple leading the fight, have been on the forefront of stricter customs and trademark/copyright protection in an effort to battle their customers' repairing their own devices. They go as far as inflating the prices they charge for damaged items to protect their profits and denying service to devices which are very obviously good to repair.

The reason for this is very simple—Apple doesn't want to be pushed out of the market by Chinese devices that rival its quality. They want their profit margins to stay as high as possible.

After all, who would buy a computer monitor stand that costs $999 when they could buy the *exact same item* (sans the Apple branding) for $40, shipping included?

Then there's obviously tax evasion. What's to stop anyone from going on a trip around the world, making a bunch of bank accounts and registering their business in Hong Kong, while running it completely online?

Nothing. In this day and age, entrepreneurs, companies, and individuals could spend, say, low five figures on a vacation and set up businesses across the world, creating structures which allow for 0 percent taxation.

Getting Disruption on Your Side

Of course, most billion-dollar chains are already aware that just enough of their product—children's clothing, towels, light fixtures, boxes of cereal—is bought online that they would be leaving money on the table if they were to ignore that 10 percent of the overall retail market. Most national stores have working e-commerce sites of their own now. But these ventures are often vestigial, almost strategic afterthoughts.

It is easy to understand why a Bed Bath & Beyond or PetSmart would be reluctant to divert in-store customers to a website, even one that ultimately feeds their own bottom line. These chains thrive on impulse buys that expand the average basket. The online shopper doesn't traipse down the tempting dog toy aisle on the way to the corner of the store that sells dog food. The online shopper types his target product into the search bar, selects his preferred brand, and checks out.

In any event, if floor traffic falters, fixed overhead costs start to spiral in on themselves, making it more attractive for management in the short term to surrender the online 10 percent to web-only rivals.

Others are pursuing a longer-term approach as they slim down their expensive store footprints and transition their sales mix toward a leaner brick-and-mortar environment.

Look to Staples and Office Depot for relative success stories. Between them, these companies conquered the national office supply category by outbuilding every viable competitor. Regional chains and independent stationery shops are gone now.

Now the survivors are happy to phase out hundreds of stores, shift other territories to smaller concepts and run the rest of the nation's specialty office supply business online. Shoppers can still travel a reasonable distance to browse the aisles, ask questions and pick up orders, but the primary cash register is on the web.

The remaining stores essentially become "showrooms," which is a term that has a lot of currency in evolutionary retail discussions right now but really goes back to the era of catalog giants like JCPenney and Sears.

In a showroom model, shoppers can interact with the floor samples as much as they like. You can test an appliance, try on the clothes, play with the toys. If the merchandise you want is in store inventory, you can pay for it and take it home. Otherwise, the store pushes you toward the chain's site, where you can order your stuff and get it shipped in a few weeks.

Stores are leaner in terms of inventory and can focus on products that benefit from on-site experimentation. And in terms of the overall bottom line, it becomes less urgent to maintain so many stores as active points of sale because the web presence no longer implicitly competes with the stores themselves.

Web and showrooms complement each other, and competitors are thrown back on the defensive. At least, that's the goal.

Maybe 50 to 60 percent of the country still goes to the store to look at the clothes, then goes home to check prices and push the button on that basis. Others will compare deals against online-only vendors right there on the sales floor, and if they find a better price on the web, they'll order it via their phone.

In general, the more generic the category, the harder it is for online rivals to steal sales from in-store shoppers. Who would go to the grocery store and then place an order with Amazon Pantry to have the exact same box of cereal delivered next-day? Books, sporting goods, vitamins, cosmetics, high-end electronics: these products are highly branded and easy to search for online. Unless it's a retailer exclusive, competition becomes a matter of convenience and price.

The less money is on the table, the bigger a factor convenience becomes. Radio Shack died because most of its core merchandise was cheap, generic, and convenience-oriented. People who need any old broadband cable aren't picky about where they buy it. As Amazon moved toward faster and faster delivery cycles, it was no longer worthwhile to drive to the local cable store.

Deep discount chains like Dollar Tree on the other hand are not going anywhere. There will probably always be a place for what amounts to a convenience store model, and as long as the products are cheap, online ordering and delivery will not be a category killer. When you're in one of these stores, you want it now. Amazon can't do that yet, although that's why it's starting its own automated convenience store chain (see Chapter Five.)

Williams-Sonoma and Restoration Hardware, on the other hand, have established lines of exclusive merchandise. If you want their wares to update your kitchen, you either have to go to a store or to the company's site to get what you want. Whichever way you decide, the company wins.

Don't rule out manufacturers like Ralph Lauren and Nike bypassing retail entirely to sell direct to their loyal brand audience. A manufacturer website can provide a rich online shopping experience as well as any store chain. As a bonus, the spread between the manufacturer suggested retail price and cost is even better when it comes to weighing the margins. Shopify is the company that makes those stores happen.

One day we may see a world of branded, direct online retail, and "stores" will be limited to a mix of upscale showrooms—think Apple stores—and big-box convenience for everything else.

But with that in mind, Walmart is executing very well on its online efforts. The site is surprisingly robust, especially when it comes to supporting the company's push into the supermarket space. Shipping is free on mid-sized to large orders, and Walmart of all companies knows how to keep the price point profitable while starving everyone else who wanted that sale.

And in between, we are seeing traditional department stores evolve. I am watching Macy's and Nordstrom as leaders here. The stores have already been built and are ready to serve as showrooms. But as inventory tightens and overrun sales push back to the website, these companies have a lot of room to hang onto their market position on a more profit-able basis.

As long as companies like Kohl's keep trying to reinvent themselves by making overtures to upstarts like At Home, the game isn't over. At Home isn't an online player at all. This isn't like Walmart paying $3 billion (six times revenue) two years ago to absorb Jet.com in order to make a credible challenge to Amazon online. This is adding 180 special-ized home furnishing stores—as brick-and-mortar as it gets—to the existing 1,100-store footprint. It's an injection of more vibrant retail concepts, curated merchandise, and sales culture into a tired, old-school model.

On the surface, it's barely enough to move the needle. Last year was the first time that At Home did more than a billion dollars in sales. Kohl's still books nineteen times that much revenue across the chain, so simply bolting on the additional transactions isn't really a strategic win.

But unlike the department store, At Home is growing fast, boosting its sales 22 percent last year. That's the win. Amazon only expanded its share of the category 20 percent over the same time period. At Home is disrupting its chosen market segment faster than the Jeff Bezos machine, and it's doing it without relying too heavily on online sales to accelerate the process. That's the kind of stock we love. Whether it gets acquired now or later, it's going to make some forward-looking Old Retail execu-tive very happy.

Who else is on my radar? Factoring out restaurants and auto sales, it's another story. U.S. retail activity expanded 0.8 percent last year so the growth bar for the sector as a whole is low. Any chain that boosted its sales more than that is a winner disrupting shopping habits enough to steal share from slower competitors

Don't be fooled by that low overall percentage benchmark. The consumer economy is so vast that even 0.8 percent in fresh sales across the entire landscape translates to more than $200 billion for the winners to carve up. Granted, $63 billion shifted online, but brick-and-mortar still got more than $2 for every $1 that went to Amazon and its smaller counterparts.

And brick-and-mortar is extremely fragmented. Even $200 million can make a huge difference for next-generation chains that are still trying to score their first billion-dollar year. Naturally it's barely a rounding error for Walmart or Amazon, which need to grab $2 billion of the $200 billion pool just to give Wall Street 1 percent of growth. But we aren't looking at them right now.

Costco barely makes the grade. It expanded its sales $12 billion last year for 8 percent growth. That's nowhere near Amazon territory, but for entrenched brick-and-mortar, it's a great start. Lululemon is tiny but coming up fast. Its 14 percent sales growth only added up to $600 million. While hardly a dent in the giants' profiles, it feels really good for shareholders.

Ulta is right behind, adding $1 billion to its cosmetic sales last year for a 12 percent growth rate. We're getting close to Amazon territory now in terms of growth even if the numbers are nowhere near the same scale. That's all right. We don't want scale; we want dynamism. Five Below is also worth mentioning. Again, though tiny by Amazon standards, its 21 percent growth spurt only translates into 300 million in real dollars. Its youth-oriented discount stores are beating Amazon on that level. This is where the real action is on Main Street, even if it's starting small.

I could name a few other companies, niche-oriented brands, where even $100 million moves the needle in a big way. But you get the idea. Size is irrelevant; speed and sizzle are what matters. And there's plenty of sizzle to go around.

Figure that Amazon captured 26 percent of all new retail dollars last year. Walmart got an anemic 2 percent share, and Costco claimed 5 percent of the pool. Factor out the slow-growth names that I've only alluded to in passing (looking at you, Walgreens), and there's easily $100 billion left for the disruptors to capture. That's a boom. I'm willing to chase it down into some mighty small stocks until we've squeezed all the profit we can out of their business models. Are you?

Unintended Consequences

So what's up with the full parking lots? For many legacy chains, I think the showrooms represent too large a drain on overhead compared to the incremental benefits of remaining relevant in a mobile shopping universe. Others are making the transition better, routing in-store shoppers to the corporate web stores and suggesting delivery as part of standard operating procedure.

This is nothing revolutionary in the grand scheme of retail. It's how catalog operations like JCPenney and Sears flourished, and ultimately why they built out their brick-and-mortar stores in the first place. People wanted to see the stuff in the catalog before they placed the order. Buying in-store and taking a shopping bag home wasn't the target.

I can't help but notice that Amazon, the online behemoth, is technically classified as a "catalog retailer." That's its legacy. As Amazon conquers category after category, it adds catalogs. The site is full of hardware now. Consumer electronics. Clothing. Household products, even packaged food. It's the top showroom-free retailer right now, offering a completely virtual shopping experience.

But today's category killer can't get complacent. Teen apparel is notoriously resilient in the face of online competition because younger shoppers love the tactile experience of seeing how the clothes look and feel. Shopping is a verb at that age, so even though this is the screen-grasping, "digital native" generation, some pockets of the mall are alive and well. I can't help but notice that sales at clothing boutiques are still rising even though apparel sales in the department chains are in free fall.

This dichotomy is particularly evident during back-to-school season in the children's clothing sector. More than half of all parents make an extra visit to apparel chains between late July and early September. If this year is anything like the past, we might expect to see billions spent on new outfits for the K–college crowd.

Teenagers are notoriously impulsive when it comes to clothing choices, but younger kids tend to default to what their parents pick out. Kids don't have credit cards and can't shop online for themselves. Parents are increasingly happy to put together a new outfit by looking at the pictures online and estimating the fit.

Category by category, mall by mall, the threat is real. Online competitors have driven chain bookstores, electronics dealers, and record stores to extinction. They keep tightening the pressure on everyone else, from the neighborhood supermarket to upscale houseware boutiques.

But Wall Street wrote the mall off a decade ago. All the highly compensated people who run brick-and-mortar retail chains have had years to pivot their store concepts and merchandise mixes to get out from under Amazon's lethal shadow. Boutiques keep the malls alive, making investors a surprising amount of money on what should be a dying sector.

Amazon covets the showroom. Part of the reason it bought Whole Foods was because Bezos wanted to capture a slice of the grocery category, and people just aren't ready to buy tomatoes sight unseen. We definitely aren't ready to trust tomatoes shipped from a central warehouse, arriving after at least two days of abuse on a mail truck. The stores function as staging areas for the local delivery teams. Showing off the perfect produce is a bonus.

Amazon keeps flirting with physical stores. It supports a brick-and-mortar book chain. Its new convenience stores will expand its footprint even further. The 2,800 Amazon Lockers give third-party merchants a place to get their packages into the fulfillment system on the way to their final destinations. And with Kohl's signing up to act as a return center, the odds are good that Amazon will start using those stores as showrooms for whatever it really wants to promote.

The Bottom Line for Early Adopters

Malls are not dying. Developers who remembered the disasters of 2008–09 didn't exactly rush to overpopulate the countryside with new retail space. Supply of new shopping centers has tracked demand to the point where overall vacancies are now below the record lows we saw in 2006, as an ill-fated building boom kicked into gear. While it took years to absorb all those hundreds of millions of square feet, that process finally looks complete.

New building is tracking behind new leases and even cautious landlords are actually raising rents from tenants who believe in their concepts and have the money to pay. With $128 billion in construction loans coming due in the new year, the cash should help fend off a wave of bankruptcies. In the meantime, the stores have plenty of life left in them.

They're full of restaurants. If Amazon were a restaurant, would you eat there? With roughly one eatery for every three hundred U.S. residents, Wall Street is right to worry about the American stomach not being big enough for every ambitious chain. But even with so many national brands competing to serve each meal, it's clearly a boom.

CHAPTER ELEVEN

2021: A SPACE ODYSSEY

Modern warfare is information warfare. The side with the best information and the clearest view of the battlefield wins. The question is how far up the battlefield goes today. Every nation wants safety for its armed forces. Information warfare will reduce military and civilian casualties and facilitate quick resolutions, minimizing the destruction and human suffering brought about by war.

In the short term, even the chaos of warfare generates Big Data patterns. And those patterns afford command and control. No longer will squads and platoons need to rely on slow and tedious communication channels. Enemy positions, armaments, IED locations, and identification data will all be streamed into combatants' awareness in real time.

Imagine a situation where a Marine is walking down the road, and then for no apparent reason, ducks for cover. He didn't hear or see anything happen. But a platoon a mile away noticed a sniper perched on a hill, looking in his direction.

Now ponder the view from space.

From Earth to Orbit

Forget about the "Space Force" for a moment. The wars of tomorrow will be fought on Silicon battlefields closer to home, and as I plot the latest earnings reports of companies like Microsoft and Amazon, it's clear that Silicon Valley needs to step up to the future.

After all, the world needs high-tech help. The map of geopolitical hot spots is getting crowded, with North Korea emerging on the global stage, Venezuela braced for a full-fledged humanitarian crisis, Iran on the brink, and on and on. It's gotten to the point where French warships test the Taiwan Strait, and nobody even has time to blink.

That's the kind of world where vast amounts of money start chasing anyone who comes up with a way to help governments achieve their strategic goals, projecting power while keeping civilian populations safe.

The Martian, the 2015 movie starring Matt Damon, presents the idea that a person could be left behind on Mars and survive. The film is a work of fiction, but remember the adage, if you can dream it, you can do it? I think there is something to it. The advancement of technology and increased knowledge of asteroid mining will make Mars missions possible.

Astronauts landed on the Moon fifty years ago. In fifty short years, we have pushed past the lunar landing toward the prospect of living on Mars. Ever since the days of Galileo and Charles Messier's classification of nebulae in the 1700's, stargazers have been looking up at the sky for inspiration and in hopes of exploration. By the year 2050, it would not be surprising for explorers to travel to Mars (especially with the increasing number of billionaires who could fund it), and for human settlements to crop up on the Red Planet. Governing in space will undoubtedly be a whole new world for geopolitics.

While it's great to hear that a further push into space is still on the administration's radar (so to speak), the news so far is as much flare as fire. The Space Force is starting with a $500 million annual budget, reflecting budget sensitivity at the Pentagon.

Generals can brag that this is 0.07 percent of the $750 billion defense outlay. It costs about $60 million to launch a single satellite, so the Space

Force allotment won't stretch that far. Space Force in itself won't move any investment needles, either. Let's say Lockheed Martin (LMT) captured that entire added spend: all $500 million would not add a full percentage point to their revenue.

Where this does get exciting is the civilian commercial applications. Buried in the vice president's comments about Space Force was a reminder that the real financial push into space is coming from Department of Commerce and not Defense. Commerce is the department that's almost ready to unveil a next-generation orbital navigation database as part of a dedicated effort to tame the "new Wild West." That project goes live at the end of June. From there, Wilbur Ross wants to promote the domestic satellite industry, which means extra visibility for LMT as well as Northrop Grumman and Boeing.

It could also be a GameChanger for MAXAR Technologies, which owns the old Loral Space Systems business. Here at a run rate around $2 billion, it will not take much stimulus to fast-track their growth again. Ross insists that the space business is primed to go ballistic in the next twenty years. His low estimate for growth is 5 percent compounded per year but real growth could ultimately go at double that rate. Over a twenty-year window, that's huge. This is where I'd look for real impact on portfolios.

And of course those satellites need monitoring. I'm still a fan of Intelsat as the military orbital network of choice. Of course that company now also supports a lot of civilian communications, which raises a crucial point: if Commerce leads the way, the real conquest of space will revolve around 5G, spectrum allocation, remote sensing, weather, and above all else, making sure that every device on the Internet of Things knows its position at all times.

Safe autonomous vehicles need better navigation systems than today's GPS can provide. That's an opportunity. As Ross says, "money is key" not only to the orbital leap but to the investors putting up the capital and accepting the risk in exchange for what could be truly stellar rewards in decades to come.

Trade Wars Can Be Won

As barriers rise around some international borders, of necessity goods and services find other routes to their ultimate destinations. Oil keeps moving from wells to refining plants and ultimately to consumers. Tarrifs or no tarrifs, China still needs to eat—even if their food has to come from abroad to replace crops and livestock damaged by pests and disease. Americans and American companies still need products from overseas. If historical sources close, people create new supply chains elsewhere.

Trade has been an overhang on corporate outlooks since the 2018 downswing, and most companies exposed to truly crippling tariffs have either shifted suppliers or will simply pass on higher import fees to their customers.

Some will do both. Look at what Dollar Tree is doing. They've shifted their seasonal merchandise supply contracts away from China and are now experimenting with raising their average price point beyond the symbolic dollar. Whatever these companies do, they aren't sitting passively, watching the headlines and waiting for the world to end. They're anticipating developments, planning for the worst while remaining open to the very real prospect that we'll see a trade truce if not a complete breakthrough soon. China wants a deal. We want a deal.

The Information Battlefield

In Ancient Greece and Rome, the power of intelligence was prized. Intelligence, not only in the common sense of intellect, but also in the martial meaning, knowing more than one's enemy does. In fact, no civilization in the ancient world relied more on espionage than the Romans. Caesar famously had a sprawling intelligence network throughout Rome, carefully watching his enemies. Rome deployed spies and patrols to their borders and partnered with foreign allies.

This allowed them to maintain an empire which followed the rule of law and maintained authority. In more recent history, the breaking of the Enigma code was critical in ensuring victory against the Nazi threat. Breaking the encryption on Nazi communications allowed the Allies to properly address future threats and gain both a strategic and tactical advantage on both the Eastern and Western fronts.

Wartime espionage has evolved with the available modes of communication—from drums and signal flags to carrier pidgeons and telegraphs to GPS-enabled devices. Modern conflicts rely on ever more sophisticated communications technology.

It is no surprise that the intelligence community is on the forefront of communications developments. There's a multitude of innovations which have come to the surface in recent years, and to cover them all here would be an exceedingly daunting task, but one of the main innovations in intelligence and military communications is encryption. Onion routing has been freely available to anyone in the world for a good time now. It was first developed by the U.S. Navy and later completed by the Defense Advanced Research Projects Agency and patented by the U.S. Navy in 1998.

Since then, it has become the go-to solution for the intelligence community to transmit information in an anonymous and encrypted manner over the World Wide Web. Security protocols practically guarantee anonymity and privacy, allowing communications to bypass enemy censors. Examples include China's "Great Firewall" and Kazakhstan's recent employment of man-in-the-middle attacks on the "Hyper-text transfer protocol secure" (https) protocol, denying all privacy to its citizens.

Another innovation in modern warfare has been compromising hardware vendors. It's common knowledge that Microsoft's Windows operating system (going as far back as 1999) has NSA backdoors, which allow the NSA to access any information stored on Windows-based computers. That was just the beginning. In 2007, the NSA began the PRISM program in the wake of the Protect America Act under Bush. Since then, they have built relationships with major Internet companies, such as Google, Skype, Microsoft, Yahoo, and other smaller companies.

Among the program's soft targets, we can find Venezuela, aiming at their military and oil; Mexico's narcotics trade; energy sources; internal security; and political affairs, narcotics, and human trafficking in Colombia. The program involves the ability to collect all kinds of information—emails, chats, videos, documents, phone calls, and metadata, such as when someone got a notification, where they were when that happened, which mobile telecommunications tower their cell phone was connected with, and more.

Cybernetic Espionage

There's also the matter of cyber warfare proper, including hacking, data extraction, and malicious intrusion into computer networks and systems. The stakes of even a small attack are stunning; it's no wonder that the NSA is on the bleeding edge of security development. Consider for a moment a nuclear reactor. It requires meticulous care, 24/7 monitoring and reporting, periodic adjustments, maintenance, cooling, appropriate shielding—all supported by high-tech systems. What would happen if the ventilation system failed and didn't report its failure on the technician's computer screen?

In 2010, news broke that there had been incidents, including a "serious nuclear accident" in the Natanz nuclear facilities in Iran. Apparently in that uranium enrichment facility, centrifuge operational capacity had dropped by 30 percent over the span of a year. That is a serious matter. The attack was ingenious. The virus didn't corrupt data or shut systems down. It simply accelerated the control system that the centrifuges relied on, speeding them up and slowing them down until their aluminum shells ruptured at 1000 rotations per minute.

The facility was literally killed by a catalyst. In the wake of automation, where cars are computer-controlled and soon will be able to drive themselves, copycat tactics are a real concern. What's to stop an ingenious team from creating computer viruses which cause physical damage to infrastructure without an armed assault?

Imagine the chaos that would reign if New York City's traffic lights were to go out. Some smart cookies might be able to drive without guidance, but only a few hacked self-driving cars would be enough to cause massive congestion. This would break all logistics, stranding people all over the city. Freight would stop coming in. New York famously has only two days' worth of food on the shelves at any given moment. It's a scary thought.

It's reassuring that we have the world's best security researchers working for our great nation. The power grid can be hardened against outside attack. For example, I was pleasantly surprised by how well the utilities in Texas managed to keep most of the lights on during Hurricane Harvey. Go back five to ten years, and that power grid would have buckled, taking down the infrastructure of modern life—water pumps, communications, electric cars—with it.

This time, amidst some of the worst urban flooding in modern history, 96 percent of the primary grid stayed lit. A week later, uptime was back up above 99.7 percent. Granted, that was still thousands of customers without power, but compared to what we saw in the wake of storms like Katrina and Sandy, it was a miracle.

The grid has gotten a lot smarter. It's getting smarter and more resilient year by year. Those who piled into the hype a decade ago are only now reaping the rewards now that the buzz has become a real business. That's how we tend to play these themes: cutting out the speculative all-or-nothing phases in favor of patiently building a position, maybe locking in a little profit along the way when the froth gets too far ahead of the fundamentals.

Right now most of the key players renovating the grid are still relatively small companies. Itron is only barely in the small-cap Russell 2000, while Roper Technologies and Digi International are even earlier in their growth cycle, so there's still plenty of time to let the story mature. Naturally, infrastructure that nature destroys will be rebuilt with the most updated technologies, so storm-threatened communities are looking at a fast upgrade once the clouds recede. If a visionary infrastructure package from Washington accelerates the process, there's a chance the grid will light up on our screen in more than a theoretical capacity. For now, we watch and wait for the future to arrive.

Hearts, Minds, and Propoganda Gold Mines

The same technologies used by the military and intelligence will soon be hitting the civilian market. This means that advertising, marketing, and the influence of social media on business will only grow. With Facebook being part of these programs, they already have the technology to influence the masses and sway political events.

We know the technology exists. It's just a matter of seeing who will find a way to deploy it. So it's a matter of playing the Gold Rush game, not investing in ads and buying them from these platforms, but putting money into the infrastructure and computer wizardry which makes this possible in the first place.

Meanwhile, we've seen most people reduce themselves to the lowest common denominator. That's just how groups operate, and now we see brands and companies attempting to leverage that for profit. Good for them. If only they knew what we know: the secrets of targeted, effective MindWar. Look at any list of companies the NSA associates with. They're almost all on the bleeding edge of their industries. They're not slacking.

And they succeed, because their marketing and sales processes are founded on those immortal principles. One can try forcing an idea all day without result—but when you find the right crowd, it'll immediately get traction and fling a business forward. Hopefully a business you've invested in!

There are also drawbacks. With surveillance from government and private interests casting a wider and wider net, we all lose privacy. Even something as simple as a phone call is not truly private. The NSA is known to collect every bit of information which crosses the American border, and their supercomputers sift through the data for anything that might endanger national security.

There are already companies that specialize in extracting that data, in collecting everything they can about everyone they can. And then they sell that information to, among others, private investigators. But it gets worse. Consider LinkedIn, an online networking platform for professionals. It's great, right?

If you go on anyone's profile, you can see what they look like, where they live, where they work, their skills, assignments, friends, and co-workers. That is dangerous information, and it's all self-contributed! Nobody holds a gun to these people's heads when they publish all that information online. But it creates a lot of problems. What's to stop someone from scraping that information, pickpocketing someone for their Social Security number, and then running large-scale scams with their stolen identity?

Identity theft is a major problem right now, and whichever company wins the government contract for increasing security is going to stay in business for a long, long time. What if a hospital gets hacked? What if a government agency gets hacked? There are incredible profits to be made for those who have solutions for these vulnerable industries.

Information warfare makes it hard to trust the media. Not only is their funding often hidden through shell companies, but they are also people. They don't want to get fired, they have families to feed. And a lie here and there, a spin, a biased opinion doesn't hurt, right?

Not so. In fact, the journalistic standard has been dangerously eroded over the last few decades, and it'll only get worse until journalism is regulated properly again. Even then, there's no guarantee that our own government won't use it for their own ends.

Flashpoint: The Middle East

There's always a fresh fear factor somewhere in the global markets. For now, everything I see makes me think the U.S. economy is positioned unusually well to climb the latest wall of worry.

Start with the Strait of Hormuz, which connects the Persian Gulf and Gulf of Oman. For decades, this two-mile shipping lane has been the global economic chokepoint, with 20 percent of the world's oil supply at risk if tensions escalate.

But we don't live in the 1970s or even the 1980s anymore. Pipelines across Saudi Arabia can divert some of that at-risk oil to Red Sea outlets and from there, eager consumers in Asia and Europe will be able to keep their lights on. Here at home, North American shale can theoretically surrender enough petroleum to satisfy domestic demand. We're in a much better strategic position than we were in the 1970s.

What we can't do is export enough of our oil on our own to completely eliminate the threat. U.S. ports can export about five million barrels of oil a day. Even if the Saudis flood their pipelines and Russia taps every idle well, the world would need to replace as many as 12 million barrels a day if the Straits close. That sounds daunting, doesn't it?

The world is still swimming in strategic petroleum reserves that were topped off in the 2014–16 glut and are now standing by to smooth over any supply disruption. We're talking about 2.9 billion barrels around the world. Some countries have more and others have less, but all together there's enough oil stockpiled to cover any shortfalls for at least five to six months. Beyond that point, if the Straits aren't clear, fuel prices will spike like they did in the 1970s.

Oil markets tell me a prolonged disruption is unlikely. Futures trading doesn't reflect any question marks five to six months out or even beyond that timeframe. Instead, what we're seeing is a healthy reversion to long-term, normal pricing after the 2014–16 glut. Demand for fuel is now sufficiently aligned with supply that the risk of a shortfall is meaningful. That's good for the oil stocks. They were struggling when West Texas crude was worth less than $55 a barrel. If their output becomes a matter of global security any time soon, their reserves are going to be worth more, and their balance sheets are going to feel a lot of relief.

Energy stocks have had a rough ride over the past decade. The 2014–15 decline has easily made energy the worst-performing segment since the bull market began in March 2009, after outperforming considerably over the last decade. The reason for the decline is simple: too much oil here at home. Oil crashed from $100 to $40 in two years due to a surge in U.S. oil production. This jump in oil supply was thanks to improved drilling technology—hydraulic fracturing, or "fracking"—that allowed for the retrieval of oil from previously hard to get at locations. High prices, along with lower interest rates, made such projects economical.

Natural gas is a different market than oil. It's largely domestic and seasonal in nature, though prices of the two commodities tend to move in tandem. Gas is generally injected into storage from May to September, when little is used for home heating, and then withdrawn from storage in the months when homes are operating their heaters. Prices can be volatile throughout the winter, as an extended snap of frigid weather could drain inventories.

Through the middle part of the previous decade, people were concerned that there was a permanent shortage of natural gas in the United States and that it would become too expensive for industrial use. First in 2005 following fears of supply disruption due to Hurricane Katrina, and again in 2008 when oil rose to $130 a barrel, the price of natural gas spiked to over $12 a thousand cubic feet. Eventually, fracking eliminated all of the supply problems, and the price of natural gas hasn't reached $6 since the end of the financial crisis.

I believe we are close to a long-term bottom for both oil and natural gas, although we have hit a few false bottoms already, so the exact timing of a rally is hard to project. Given the difference fracking has made in increasing available supply to the United States, we will not see $100 a barrel for a long time, perhaps ever again, as we begin a slow but sure transition to cheaper fuels.

Silicon Valley Goes to War

The U.S. military needs the best technology partners on the planet. And as it happens, the biggest civilian technology vendors are now so big that government budgets are the only ones left that scale fast enough to keep their fundamentals moving.

Let traditional prime contractors like General Dynamics and Lockheed Martin shake. Defense is the final frontier for the civilian giants, and soon it's going to be hard to see where the Pentagon ends and Silicon Valley begins.

The latest round of bickering over the $10 billion right to run the U.S. military's cloud computing platform puts all this in sharp focus. Only civilian contractors are in the running for command of the Joint Enterprise Defense Infrastructure (JEDI) initiative. The company that wins the Pentagon's nod will effectively shift all of the most sensitive and secure military systems onto its "operating system," whether that happens to be Microsoft's Azure or Amazon's AWS Web Services platform.

IBM and Oracle coveted the prize but dropped out early. Last I heard, Alphabet was still in the running as an underdog. Only Apple, the pinnacle of civilian systems, has resisted the siren call.

After all, even amortized across a ten-year contract term, $10 billion is still a lot of money for any of these giants. For Amazon, it's enough to boost AWS growth 3 percentage points a year and create an extra 2 percentage points of profit, all off a single contract.

Microsoft's growth needle would move a similar amount if it wins the contract, which I would bet on right now because its sales team can sweeten its bid with Office and other professional software to run on the Pentagon cloud.

Amazon can't match that by offering free shipping on soap, but it points out the way JEDI is really just a trial run to see how well all the parties can work together on bigger applications.

The Pentagon's budget request for the 2020 fiscal year is in the zone of $718 billion. A tenth of that money pushed toward either the Amazon or the Microsoft cloud would send the country leapfrogging across years of anticipated organic growth, launching either company into the future in one giddy leap.

The Billionaire Space Race

There are people with ample funds and innovative minds who formed space companies for the purpose of venturing into space exploration. It could be considered the 21st century space race. A few leading players include:

Sir Richard Branson, British high-school dropout turned billionaire and tireless visionary, formed the company Virgin Galactic in 2004 with Burt Rutan (under the parent company The Virgin Group) with the intention of providing both commercial travel ("space tourism") and scientific exploration. One of the early movers, he's still in the race with a suborbital spaceplane that can take passengers on short zero-gravity jaunts or to extraterritorial space stations.

Jeff Bezos is not particularly interested in shipping items to Mars. His interests are lunar instead. The Amazon founder is not only the lead when it comes to expediently shipping items on planet Earth, but having nurtured aerospace manufacturer Blue Origin, he envisions a Moon Lander's launching by the year 2024. Talk about shooting for the moon! His website, BlueOrigin.com, goes into detail about the Moon Lander, which will be able to deliver items to the moon in order to help sustain those who explore and live there.

Elon Musk's "other company" Space-X has a $20 billion-valuation and arguably even deeper pockets. It may never go public, but as its rocket platform gets more robust, it takes a lot of pressure off satellite operators like Iridium Communications. Everyone argues that orbital launch capacity at an economically viable price is a strategic necessity for everything from GPS-enabled drones to missile defense, but unless Musk can pull it off, growth opportunities for IRDM and company look constrained at best. Again, this isn't necessarily a reason to buy the satellites—it's more of a way for the group to remain relevant.

Getting Disruption on Your Side

The traditional investment case for a more robust space presence revolves around defense. Being able to avert catastrophic asteroid impacts would help preserve everything we've already built, and creating an escape route would allow us to flee if something were to go catastrophically wrong on Earth. At its core, money spent here is all about risk management and ultimately diversifying our planetary footprint.

And from there, the story opens up to some truly transformational upsides. Capturing an asteroid for study would be a scientific windfall and a literal gold mine. NASA has greenlit a mission to investigate one space rock that appears to be made of enough precious metal to run the global economy for 130,000 years. (That's $10 quintillion in platinum, gold, and everything else that glitters.) That's just one rock out of millions.

Mountains of gold. Endless clean water. Oceans of what amounts to natural gas. Rare earth minerals for the taking. Exotic gems. People invested in technology in the past and reaped the rewards—think of the success of venture capitalists who invested in a little company called MacIntosh, now called Apple. Now space travel is the hot commodity and for good reason. You're theoretically doubling humanity's aggregate mineral and chemical wealth.

That's what Branson really wants. He's invested in Planetary Resources, a company that focuses on mineral extractions (including asteroids) in order to make Mars and the moon not only reachable, but habitable. Although he has yet to launch commercial passengers into space, approximately 600 people have already invested $80 million in the venture. Branson loves an IPO so there's a good chance we'll get to play too. Bezos and Musk may also open up to outside capital when it becomes clear that they need more cash to achieve their goals.

Diversification is definitely the way to go. I would not put all your proverbial eggs in one space capsule because the extreme challenge of opening up a new planet practically guarantees that there will be failures along the way. Even so, the rewards for success are so large that whoever raises the flag will more than adequately compensate investors with even small stakes.

My suggestion: equal allocations across every exploration company you can get into where you have any confidence at all in their ability to execute. Most will lose the space race or even flame out along the way. Maximize your odds of being in the one that wins.

Extend your research to the parent companies. For example, Amazon's performance determines how much its founder has to fund Blue Sky. After all, he'll only keep pouring cash into his personal rocket toybox as long as he has it. The rest of us can stow away for the ride, but if he gets stuck, we all get stuck.

Musk can get stuck, but for now, he promises SpaceX will be "the Tesla of commercial spaceflight," whatever that means to you. (I can't decide if I'm frightened or thrilled. Arguably the terrestrial Tesla is all the wild ride any planet can absorb.) SpaceX's primary products are the Falcon launch vehicle family and the Dragon spacecraft family, both of which currently deliver payloads into Earth's orbit.

Getting the company's reusable rockets back on the launch pad after a long pause has relit the revenue fuse, I estimate the run rate here should start at around a billion dollars, and the more rockets that blast off and return safely, the better that number should get. This new race for space may seem like a science fiction endeavor that's not suited for Wall Street, but there's serious money funding this trend that brings it closer to reality. Again, he wants to go to Mars.

Down here at home, the immediate aerospace and defense industry applications are more about risk mitigation than conquest. Start in the home, where Echo Boomers (born roughly between the mid-1970s and '90s) encompass a wide age span and a lot of life experience hidden from corporate consultants fretting about "the millennial worker." Many of these people spent time at war in the Middle East or elsewhere. They're spending their money on weapons and ammunition.

Companies like Smith and Wesson, Olin, and Sturm Ruger have held up extremely well in the wake of recent tragic events. Military millennials naturally turn to these companies in a crisis. If our world starts looking precarious, ammunition sales naturally bloom. Olin makes ammunition for Winchester and may be a logical sympathetic play here—after all, without bullets, the guns are just for show.

Then there's Digital Ally, which builds digital video imaging products used by law enforcement agencies and security. Their main products are body cameras worn by law enforcement and digital audio and visual systems built in to the rearview mirror of law enforcement vehicles. Police departments are now seeking to record evidence and protect officers, largely because of the moral outrage of Echo Boomers over perceived racial injustice by the police.

Palantir is another company that never sleeps. I've been waiting years for this Big Data company to go public. It's a cult favorite in the cloak-and-dagger world of big government, communications analysis, and surveillance, taking its name from the telepathic crystal balls used to see and communicate with distant lands in J.R.R. Tolkien's *The Lord of the Rings* universe. Co-founder Peter Thiel (who also co-founded PayPal) wants to an IPO as soon as possible but knows that he's got to wait for profitability to make a credible Wall Street debut. With some gauges of revenue growth ramping up 70 to 100 percent a year, that could happen any day now. The company's Palantir Gotham is used by counter-terrorism analysts at the U.S. Department of Defense, fraud investigators, and cyber analysts. Its other primary project, Palantir Metropolis, is used by hedge funds, banks, and financial services firms. It has also expanded its customer base to serve state and local governments, as well as private companies in the healthcare field. With a far-ranging reach, Palantir is shaping up for an impressive debut… if only we could see it coming.

A few decades ago, the military would have built its own cloud with internal resources. In the modern economy, that's a waste of resources, reinventing the wheel. Of course I'm not counting the legacy contractors out of the long-term race. Some are already growing as fast as Amazon or Microsoft according to various metrics, largely on the back of extremely lucrative existing Pentagon relationships.

After all, the vast majority of the military economy revolves around vehicles and other metal in motion: satellites, ships, aircraft, missiles, and tanks. That's still the world where Lockheed Martin, General Dynamics, and their peers cash billion-dollar checks every year.

In that crowd, stocks are relatively cheap because Wall Street would rather back a civilian fad than a fully loaded war machine. Say that Lockheed, for example, trades at sixteen times earnings at any given moment. Northrop Grumman, one of my long-term favorites, is available for under a fifteen times multiple, cheaper than the market as a whole. Granted, Northrop Grumman isn't looking at much growth before next year so it's unlikely to go ballistic any time soon, but Lockheed is expanding its bottom line as fast as Microsoft, which commands a twenty-seven times multiple.

On a pure growth-adjusted earnings basis, which stock is the smarter investment? For me, the answer is clear. But it raises a follow-up question for the Silicon Valley executives who run their companies' buyback programs. If the growth rates are equal, and another company has an inside track on the biggest technology budget in history, I'd buy its shares instead of mine. Since Lockheed trades at a 60 percent earnings discount relative to Microsoft, the choice should be obvious.

Sooner or later, Big Tech is going to buy Big Defense. It might look something like Jeff Bezos or Elon Musk acquiring an existing contractor in order to give a private rocket venture more credibility. Or it might be something more transformational. Microsoft has $130 billion in cash. Lockheed Martin, the biggest Pentagon contractor around, is a $93 billion company.

Unintended Consequences

This far out, the ramifications roll out more like a list of questions than clear results. Asteroid mining may become a highly lucrative business but how will the miners get paid? Blockchain-driven exchange units may come into their own above the sky, provided of course that there's a way to execute transactions beyond the WiFi-free interplanetary gulf. More likely the units will fork across network gaps, with specialized exchange points to negotiate the interface.

The first travelers won't find any data there but what they bring with them or build. They'll have a planet to tame. Based on the focus on STEM in schools, more students need be more prepared to map out their future college careers or vocations in aeronautics, coding, engineering, and space travel. Jobs will crop up which haven't been invented yet—on Earth, the Moon, Mars, and corners of the universe we have yet to discover.

Terrestrially, there is profit to be made in next-generation media companies that can fact-check or feed audience bias. What would happen if each channel, each station presented the news in its own, apparently divergent way, but still arrived at the same conclusions? A company able to intelligently process large amount of information and deliver scripts on time, every time, will make millions.

The Bottom Line for Early Adaptors

As we shift our sights from Earth to outer space, the future seems to be at our doorstep. Those with the dreams and the means are in the process (thanks to the billionaire space race) of making commercial space travel for consumers and goods not only possible, but actually probable.

By 2050, commercial space travel will be not be the stuff of science fiction, but quotidian reality. By that point, market forces will start driving the costs down. Think back to the evolution of mass-market airplane travel from the 1950s to today. Once upon a time this transportation category was reserved for the affluent. Now anyone with the cash for a ticket can fly. Buckle up for a rerun.

CHAPTER TWELVE

THE FINAL HUMAN FRONTIER: AN AGING WORLD

In December 2018, Finland celebrated its one-hundred-first birthday with its traditional Independence Day ball. Over half of the Nordic nation's population of 5.5 million people tuned in to watch President Sauli Niinistö greet artists, generals, hockey players, and other luminaries of Finnish life.

As always, the guests of honor were veterans and auxiliaries from Finland's wars against the Soviet Union in the early 1940s. The ninety-year-olds and centenarians were the first in the reception line, had their own dining room, and were toasted and serenaded throughout the meal. There were dozens of these ninety-five-and-overs in attendance and many of them walked up to the president (a spring chicken of only seventy) on their own two feet.

Finland has hundreds of centenarians (many older than their country) and tens of thousands of citizens over ninety years old. Life expectancy is rising for men and women, a trend echoed in Japan, Norway, China, Brazil, and other countries around the world. And in the next few decades, we are likely to live longer and do more with those extra years.

A Vision of a Long, Shared Tomorrow

China's prefecture-level city of Hezhou was established in 2002. As the first "longevity city" in the country, almost 20 percent of the population is over sixty and almost 500 of Hezhou's 2 million residents are over a hundred years old. The city has invested over CNY 20 billion in "eco-health projects" promoting life sciences and ecological construction.

Much of this investment has been focused on preserving the city's natural environment. Officials attribute their city residents' health to heavy forest cover and concentrations of trace minerals in the soil. Talks at the city's first "World Longevity Forum and Life Science Conference" emphasized the importance of focusing retirement health care on disease prevention, symptom relief, and post-rehabilitation care.

The World Economic Forum's Global Agenda Council on Aging sees a "Fourth Industrial Revolution" taking shape that should fundamentally enhance the health of older adults. The future of elder health care is mobile, real-time, and personal.

Wearable sensors and analytics already play a role in preventing one of the most significant hazards facing the elderly, falling. In 2018, Professor Bruce Schatz and the Women's Health Initiative reported on their study that used small wearable motion sensors to analyze the walking patterns of sixty-seven women over the age of sixty. They found small instabilities that accurately predicted which participants were likely to fall.

Personal health monitoring is on the way to being comprehensive, non-invasive, and ubiquitous. In a 2017 paper, Sumit Majumber explored the role smart homes can play in elderly health care. His model depicted a body sensor network of small wearables and implants tracking blood pressure, heart rate, blood glucose, EEG, ECG, and respiration rate. The information would be collected by a low-powered computer on the user's belt, then shared with smarter home systems through the home's wireless network.

Medical sensors can do more than warn about problems. "Smart pills" that signal when they have been consumed provide confirmation that elderly patients are actually receiving treatment. Proteus Digital Health embeds a one-square-millimeter sensor in a pill. The sensor is activated as the pill is dissolved, sending a signal to a battery-powered patch on the patient's torso. That signal then gets passed on to a smart-phone app.

The medicine that the pills deliver is growing more powerful as well. PRI-002 is a new drug for treating Alzheimer's disease that has been shown to eliminate toxic beta-amyloid oligomers and improve memory in mice. The drug recently passed phase one human testing for safety and will now be tested for human effectiveness.

Scientists are uncovering new drug applications in many other fields, as well. Researchers at the MD Anderson Cancer Center in Houston are reporting progress against colorectal cancer with a three-drug combina-tion that overcomes the tumor's adaptability. The immunotherapy drug Teplizumab may delay the onset of diabetes by two years.

Even older drugs are being studied for new uses. Rapamycin was derived from soil bacteria found on Easter Island in the 1960s and has been used as an antifungal and immune suppressor. New research sug-gests it may also work as an anti-aging drug that spurs a recycling process clearing faulty proteins out of cells.

It's impossible to tell which drugs being researched today will be the wonder drugs of tomorrow. But our understanding of the biochemical workings of the human body is leaping forward. The door is open for a new generation of highly effective, precisely targeted drugs and therapies.

The Generational Cycle Turns

After thirty years of increasingly personalized and effective real-time healthcare, today's fifty-year-old is likely to arrive at his or her eighties in substantially better condition than today's seniors, who are themselves already in good shape. So what is life going to be like for the senior citizen of 2050?

First and foremost, expect to see a lot more of Generation X. Born into the Baby Bust of 1965 to 1980, this generation has gotten used to being left in the shadow of the Baby Boomers and the Millennials. After a mere eight decades, though, the Xers might finally be ready to come into their own.

Generation X was born on the cusp of massive changes in technology and public policy. Xers drink and smoke less than the Baby Boomers did, though they could stand to eat less and get out of their desk chairs more. Meanwhile, the Boomers will be further down the actuarial survival curve. They may be the most numerous generation of ninety-somethings ever, but they will finally be outnumbered two to one by the survivors of Generation X.

The Millennials will still outnumber Generation X, but the Xers will have the advantage of fully matured economic and political assets. Generation X grew up with the information revolution and benefited from building a large swathe of the early Internet. Steve Jobs may have been a Boomer, but Musk, Brin, Page and Dorsey were all born in the 1970s. By 2050, Generation X will have spent years or decades as the heads of governments, corporations, and funds. The sixty-something Millennials will just be reaching their prime.

That puts Generation X in much the same position as today's Baby Boomers. The Xers will be stepping slowly out of the limelight, but their values and priorities will still be driving politics and culture. Expect more skepticism of authority (even though the Xers are the authorities and will have been for years). Expect more focus on information, less on material goods. Expect retirement communities with fewer golf courses and bingo games, but more bands and Dungeons & Dragons groups.

Society as a whole will benefit from more seniors, too. The Baby Boomers are more likely to drive this change, reorienting society one more time as they move into the later stages of life. The economy has shifted with the Boomers for decades and will continue to do so until their numbers drop from attrition. The investments being made in health care and robotics today will pay off over the next twenty years as the age group needing this care reaches critical mass.

Making Room for Accessibility

There is a movement in today's architectural community to "design for the blind." This movement embraces the idea that creating spaces that are easy for the visually-impaired to use goes much further than adding caution strips to steps or Braille to signs. Designing for the blind widens sidewalks and provides aids like tactile pavers to make navigation easier. It standardizes room layouts and provides audio cues to help blind visitors orient themselves. It prioritizes fast, affordable mass transit systems over individual cars.

Designing for people with disabilities actually makes objects and spaces more accessible for all users. The growing generation of senior citizens will need that accessibility just as much, if not more. They will be more healthy and active than their predecessors, but slower and more unsteady than they used to be.

As they have done so many times before, the aging Boomers will reconfigure the world around them to meet their needs. More ramps, fewer stairs. Larger bathrooms and lower toilets. Signs with bigger print. Larger buttons. Lower counters. Wider doors which wheelchairs can get through. More buses and assistive driving technologies. Vast swathes of physical infrastructure will change to make aging Boomers comfortable, making houses, offices, and streets more accessible to everyone.

Digital infrastructure will change as well. Elderly Boomers will need technology more than they ever did before—and unlike Generation X, they grew up without learning how to program their VCRs. Today's world of wireless networks and constant connection is geared toward ease and convenience; this emphasis will only grow in the coming years.

To be useful to older Boomers, the sensors and devices of 2030 and beyond will be voice controlled and ready for use right off the shelf. A Boomer will unbox his new phone, set the new entertainment screen on the TV table, and watch the new refrigerator or home health care robot unpack itself.

The device will do all the work itself. It will find the home network, ask its owner a few questions, listen to the answers, and auto-configure. Using an evolved descendant of Alexa or Siri, it will then follow its owner's commands. Using predictive algorithms, it will try to anticipate its owner's needs. Like perfect butlers, our phones will be part of an army of digital domestic servants tending to our every need—though because we will still be human, we will probably still be complaining about the help.

Nurses Needed, or at Least More Robots

The nursing community is already under pressure from the aging population and has found recruitment difficult due to the length of training required and the strenuous work conditions of a nurse's daily life. Elder care robots will help, but the healthcare industry has a lot of work to do if it is going to make up the shortfall.

This will not be cheap. The Finnish government is committing five million euros towards the creation of 200 university spots for nursing students in 2020–21, citing the need for skilled nursing help for the elderly. Japan has passed controversial legislation expanding its visa offerings for nurses and other foreign workers, but seems unlikely to fill its expected gap of hundreds of thousands of workers. The monthly premiums of Japan's public nursing care insurance have nearly doubled since the system was introduced in 2000, and they are expected to rise further as Japan's population ages.

The United States has not had to deal with a wave of aging citizens on Japan's scale yet, but it has a long way to go to bring its care up to the standards of other developed nations. In 2017, the Commonwealth Fund's Twentieth International Health Policy survey found the United States at or near the bottom of eleven wealthy countries in Europe and North America. Today's elderly Americans visit the doctor less and pay more in out-of-pocket costs, and the United States needs to rethink

Medicare and a host of other delivery systems to make sure its aging population is taken care of.

Care for the elderly goes beyond prevention and cures. Tomorrow's senior citizens will be healthier and more independent than ever before. Aging bodies and minds require special care. With the proportion of senior citizens rising relative to the rest of the population, there will be fewer humans to help with that care.

Enter the robots. Japan's tech-friendly culture and aging demographics have made it a leader in developing robotic care for the elderly. The country expects a gap of 380,000 specialized elder care workers by 2025 and has been racing to fill that gap with robotic assistants of all kinds.

In the Shin-tomi nursing home in Tokyo, twenty different kinds of robots help care for the residents. They provide exercise routines, help with walking and emotional support. They can be humanoid, like Pepper, which is programmed to interact with humans and read emotional states. Or they can be completely inhuman, like Resonye, a bed that can split into a wheelchair. The Japanese government treats both as robots and spent over $50 million to introduce robots into care facilities in its 2017 fiscal year.

Other countries have taken notice. Korea has over 600 companies developing domestic robots, many of which are focused on eldercare. An autonomous meal-transport robot named GoCart has been delivering meals in U.S. elder care facilities since 2014. It was created by a Korean-Swedish-American partnership.

In Finland, the Robotics and the Future of Welfare Services project (known as the ROSE Project) has taken a comprehensive look at how advances in robotics can create products and services for the welfare of an aging population. It sees a strong role for robots in providing care for seniors wanting to live in their own homes as long as possible.

In a recent report, the ROSE Project presented a number of opportunities for robots in the next five years, including delivering supplies, administering medication, and providing mobility services. Robots can provide personalized assistance for patients undergoing physical and mental therapies. They can also assist with walking and the collection of information.

Improved autonomy and communications functions in the next ten years will lead to even more breakthroughs. The ROSE Project forecasts opportunities for enhanced prosthetics, providing basic therapy to patients, and providing nursing care in dangerous or quarantined environments. The robots of 2030 will not replace nurses or doctors, but they will dramatically extend nurses' and doctors' capabilities.

The market for personal assistance robots is thriving, with hundreds of companies in Korea alone. But like the early computer market in the 1980s, it is fragmented across many designs and brands. Isaac Asimov's "U.S. Robots" has not emerged yet—and it probably won't be American when it does.

The Apple of robotics will be the company that can bring the diverse robotic solutions to people's problems under one brand. This is no easy task. Unlike computers, robotic design thrives on specialized solutions. To dominate the market, this company will need to buy up small manufacturers across the world, find enough shared components to build a supply chain and develop a consistent trade dress.

A consumer-facing company will also have to humanize its products. The robots used in Japanese elder care today have names and personalities; the elderly need someone to relate to as much as they need the care itself. Like the Walt Disney Company, the future market leader in personal robots will spend as much time building up a cast of characters as a product line.

iRobot might be able to accomplish this feat, if it can step out of its home care niche. It already has a focus on utility and personal service, not to mention an iconic brand name. Industrial robot companies like Waypoint Robotics may also be able to branch into the consumer market if they can find a consumer-friendly way to present themselves. But the market is wide open. The leading robotics company of the 2040s probably hasn't been born yet.

Getting Disruption on Your Side

Growth and shifts in elder care will impact entire economies in the United States and around the world. It will grow with the elderly population, which the United Nations estimated at 809 million in 2012, 1.13 billion by 2022 and over 2 billion by 2050. The global geriatric medicine market was estimated at $540 billion in 2015. Industry estimates suggest that it could reach $1.1 trillion by 2026. The U.S. market alone is likely to be around $350 billion by 2024.

The care services market is even larger. Industry estimates valued it at $842 billion in 2017, and it is expected to grow to $1.49 trillion in 2024. The need will likely outstrip the supply, as growth is likely to be limited by high costs in wealthy countries and lack of availability in developing countries. The global market for medical robots is dwarfed by the market for medicine and care, but industry estimates still expect it to reach $24.6 billion by 2025. That's a four-fold increase over the market of $6.6 billion in 2018.

These growing markets are the most directly affected, but increased longevity will have indirect effects on construction, fitness, media, tourism, and leisure activities. These industries may only see minor growth from the elderly, but the elderly will capture a greater share of their attention and focus.

Research into treatments for aging and aging-related conditions is exciting, but success is a moon shot. Unless you enjoy gambling, stay away from the shiny robots and wonder drugs. While the work being done in age-related medicine and technology-assisted care is certain to lead to big innovations and blockbuster products, it's almost impossible to tell which ones will even make it to the marketplace, much less become sustainable businesses. There are thousands of hardworking robot manufacturers all around the world, but most of them will fail and disappear. Likewise, most revolutionary drug therapies also fail somewhere in the testing process.

Drug companies and technology companies can be good investments in general, of course. But the decision should be based on the strength of their existing products and their overall track records in research and development. Betting on the success of a particular drug or device in development is the kind of risk that only the company itself should take. Instead of pursuing the creators of medical advances, look to invest in the distributors of new technology and cures. Hospitals and health care networks will identify the successful products and profit no matter who creates them.

The elderly of the next thirty years will need health care, assistance, and entertainment. They will also be members of a generation that grew up with personal technology. The companies and organizations that accommodate their needs with individualized, easy-to-use solutions will be the shining lights of 2050.

In contrast, the big names in elder medical care are probably the big names of today. GlaxoSmithKline, Novartis, Pfizer, and the other big companies all have active projects in the geriatrics medicine market. These companies are well aware of the future size of their market and the number of problems that are available to solve. They also have the resources for the long-term research necessary to develop new drugs and therapies.

Even when they're not hands-on with a new breakthrough, pharmaceutical companies are likely to play a role in financing the people who are. In 2016, Pfizer partnered with Indiegogo in a search for entrepreneurs with "innovative products to support healthy living as we age." The company awarded $50,000 of funding to Alchemi Labs, a startup that uses radiant barriers to build heat-reflecting sun hats.

Aging Baby Boomers and Generation Xers will have the time, money, and vigor to pursue active entertainment, fitness, and travel. Active seniors could be a huge market for fitness clubs and manufacturing companies. In Finland and the neighboring countries, it's not uncommon to see eighty-somethings charging down a snow-covered park trail, pumping a Nordic walking pole in each hand for balance and aerobic exercise. Health club companies like Welcyon are already focusing on customers over fifty, featuring one-on-one coaching, "smart" equipment, and a "non-intimidating" setting.

The cruise and package tour industries will continue to prosper, but Generation X is used to doing for itself. Airbnb is already in an excellent position to offer authentic, individualized experiences to a generation that will soon have more resources and time for long-term travel.

The most rewarding investment plays are in how to improve quality of life for the aging, not in extending lifespan. The retirees of the next few decades will have the time, health, and wealth to do more of what they enjoy. Airlines will do good business with seniors, especially if suborbital travel technology makes jaunts across the planet quick and affordable. Airbnb will continue to build long-term relationships with its customers and should grow for years when it finally decides to go public. Casinos, video game companies, and sports merchandisers will all be working hard to soak up entertainment dollars from the oldest sector of the population.

Real estate and construction are also appealing investment prospects. Builders with retirement community operations like PulteGroup and Lennar have an edge in customizing communities and infrastructure to meet the needs of active senior citizens. Big commercial construction companies like Skanska are making building accessibility a priority in their developments.

Unintended Consequences

The Millennial generation will benefit from longer lives and better health... eventually. For the next few decades, they may find their paths blocked by the generations in front of them. Some are already having an impact in business and politics, of course. But Generation X is just beginning to come into its own today, as the Baby Boomers begin taking a step back. It will be a while before the next generation gets its turn as CEOs, senators, and president.

Youth culture is likely to take a hit as the media caters to the interests of an older audience. So are educational and social services for youths. Declining enrollment is already taking a toll on colleges and universities, with Harvard Business School professor Clayton Christensen predicting that 50 percent of them may close in the next decade. Christensen's prediction may be extreme, but many schools will have to change their business models. Colleges and universities may find themselves focusing on new offerings for older adults seeking to go back to school.

One last area of investment may seem a bit like a snake eating its own tail, but people who live longer will need more help managing their retirement funds. Financial firms like Fidelity Investments, Vanguard, and Charles Schwab will have plenty of work making sure their clients' assets continue to support their lifestyles.

And 1980s culture is poised for yet another comeback. The Star Wars generation was the last generation to grow up before the fragmentation of mass culture into hundreds and then thousands of niche channels. The characters and stories of Generation X's childhood still have wide recognition, and the Xers will soon have grandchildren to share them with. Star Wars, the Transformers, and the Terminator will be back— only this time it will be in virtual reality, and they'll be fighting Arnold Schwarzenegger with lightsabers on the shoulder of Optimus Prime.

We're All Going To Be Early Adopters

Ever since Methuselah made headlines, we have been fascinated with the prospect of living longer. We read stories about centenarians, skimming down the page looking for the answer to the inevitable question, "How did you do it?" Today, many admire long-lived societies like Japan and the Nordic countries and try to identify the practices that boost their life expectancies above average. Is it the fishy diet? Is it the ice hole swimming? What's the secret?

Now we are on the cusp of one of the biggest changes in the human experience. We are unlocking the biochemical and biomechanical secrets of longevity. When the human condition is no longer circumscribed by threescore years and ten, everything changes. There will be challenges. We will live longer, but we'll still be aging. We will walk a little slower, see a little more dimly, lose our hair and our hearing. Today's scientific advances are giving us more time, not a draught from the fountain of youth.

We will need more care. We will need the wider sidewalks, the larger print, the ramps, and the memory aids. We will need to restructure the spaces we live in to accommodate more people who are a little bit frail. This will not be cheap or convenient, but it will provide opportunities to do meaningful work, to make life better and more accessible for everyone. We will also have the chance to fully realize the gift of more time.

The prime of our lives will last longer, giving us more opportunities to lead, contribute to society, and build wealth. We will retire with sufficient health and resources to enjoy the activities we were putting off until retirement. We can look forward to third and fourth acts—to continuing our education, volunteering for the causes we believe in, or playing with great-grandchildren.

And while the generations behind us may occasionally get frustrated because we just... keep... hanging around... they'll have the luxury of growing up a little more slowly. They can take their time building their skills, their careers, their families. They will know that they have plenty of time ahead of them too. We'll be their living proof.

GRABBING THE BULL BY THE HORNS: CHANGE YOUR GAME TO MAKE MILLIONS

There's a lot of disruption on the way. I can't wait to harness it on our behalf. These technologies don't dominate my portfolio yet because they still need another year or two to mature. My subscribers have generally taken their profits within twenty-three weeks on average, so buying further out would only tie up their cash for longer periods and distract them from the companies that are making money in the here and now.

There's also the question of risk. The further a company is from realizing its commercial vision, the higher the odds that something will go wrong in the meantime, delaying the profit window or slamming it shut permanently. Some bright ideas will remain science fiction. That's why we don't play speculative names here: a lot can go wrong with any business plan between now and 2025, even more so when you're juggling timelines that span decades. Think of the companies that bet big on asteroid mining and nanotech fifteen to twenty years ago. Where are they now?

There may not be one single event, public demand, or technological breakthrough that we can point to and say, "Here is where it began." Constant development in many areas will progress to the point where we can look outside, see them moving, and say, "Here they are!" It is likely to be an evolution across many aspects.

From an investment strategy perspective, go long on the big aggregators first and then circle back around to the most exciting small names. The giants' economies of scale will keep them on top for a long time, and while they will not produce enormous returns, they seem likely to produce steady positive returns. Once you have the base covered, spread a little cash out among start-ups trying to develop applications that produce this data, according to your intuition about whether the thing they're offering to consumers is something you find compelling. You'll miss more than you'll hit, but you may hit big.

Long-term bets on FAANG, or at least Facebook, Amazon, and Google, seem to me to be a decently good idea. None of these are going to make you spectacularly rich quickly, but they're all good long-term investment vehicles given their reach.

Keep an ear out for regulatory burdens changing in various fields, finance and healthcare being two of the most obvious. Also look for analytics companies that are, in effect, using unregulated data as a more-or-less effective proxy for regulated data. Even if the numbers are hidden, a good machine learning algorithm should be able to extrapolate with a good rate of success from data you can legally ask about. Companies that facilitate that process make good investment opportunities.

Otherwise, the best advice I can offer here is that you should look for companies that provide a product or service that you would like to have and would pay for yourself, either in cash or in personal data. When you find one you like, which seems like it might be able to deliver, kick in some money. Repeat this process, and maybe one or two of the horses you backed will come in. Because market outcomes are so unpredictable in this space, hedging your risk by betting small and wide is, in my opinion, the sanest way to invest.

Don't put all your eggs in one basket, no matter how exciting that basket is. Even if someone has a really spiffy product and a good monetization strategy, there's an awful lot of contingency between a good idea and a nice initial product, and success. Even if the rest of the world finds the product you're using in exchange for your data as compelling as you do, as soon as a technology breaks out, the developers have painted a target on themselves. Since their success was probably at least in part a product of rushing their consumer-facing application into the market at the expense of securing their collected data, there's an excellent chance that their monetization will be derailed by theft of their data the instant they begin to show real signs of success.

Avoid investing in anything that everyone is already talking about. There are no leading lights in companies producing telemetry sources for ubiquitous computing, for example. By the time you hear about the company because it's causing buzz among its customers, it's too late to make a spectacularly good investment in them. Another example: The fitness tracker peak has passed, the market has consolidated, and you're not going to get spectacular results out of it now. If it has already hit the mass market, all the bets that matter are already in.

The obvious strategy is to find companies that:

a) have monetization plans that are clearly built around selling their collected data at a price that will provide profit but be low enough to be attractive to buyers

b) are offering a service to their end-users that sounds compelling enough to convince those users to give up their data in exchange for the service

c) seem to have enough technical acumen to make it plausible that they could pull off offering the service, and

d) have a reasonable enough security story that it's not immediately clear that if they ever were to start becoming successful, their database would instantly appear on the Dark Web for a much lower price than they were trying to charge.

None of these things is going to be obvious to investors, even professional/institutional ones. Companies have huge incentives to make c) and

d) appear legitimate to investors, and there's very little way to test them for truth before kicking in the money.

However, I recognize that a little science fiction adds spice and long-term focus to any growth-oriented investment strategy, so I'd like to leave you with two more thoughts. One is thematic. The other is more philosophical, I guess you could call it strategic. If all goes well, you'll start seeing them both become part of the discussion as the 2010s wind down and the long future gets close enough to actively trade.

There's A New Reality Coming... But When?

I recently saw a glossy advertisement for a virtual computing environment from software company Autodesk. The company is still around. The magazine was from 1989, which tells you just how long the dream of special goggles that project an immersive digital world has been circulating around Silicon Valley.

The quarter century of commercial trial and error that followed also serves as a bracing reminder of how long it can take for a moonshot technology to pay off for investors, when it reaches the market at all. Autodesk never brought its goggles-and-all system to the market in its original form. Instead, the company rebranded the rendering tools that it needed to generate those virtual spaces as engineering software, launching the industry we now call computer-assisted design and manufacturing in the process. The goggles remained a historical curio for other high-tech players to experiment with.

Now, of course, Alphabet/Google has its Glass, and Facebook is selling Oculus Rift. It's great that they're putting their goggles forward, but I'm not convinced yet that it's worth paying a significant premium on either stock. For one thing, both approaches to virtual reality create passive, entertainment-oriented relationships with the user. Very few people are using their headsets to create new content in the way that Autodesk opened its system to the architects and engineers. This means that until a library of professional VR content is available, Oculus Rift in particular is really just an expensive novelty while Glass boils down to a new type of portable camera.

Think about how 3-D televisions have stagnated over the last decade in the absence of must-see movies that require a special screen and glasses to get the full experience. Avatar came out a full seven years ago and there just wasn't any coherent follow-through, no "killer app" driving technophiles to make the leap. From recorded video to game consoles, the platform that gets a critical mass of content together first tends to become dominant while others fall by the high-tech wayside: VHS conquered Beta, DVD outmaneuvered laserdiscs, Nintendo and Microsoft drove Sega machines out of living rooms everywhere.

We need to find a company that either develops that kind of content or develops the tools to help users do it on their own. In other words, we need to find the first virtual game studio—the initial VR titles will probably look more like games than movies because there's less initial risk of backing the wrong platform—or the next AutoDesk. That's a tough target right now, but I think it's worth looking at what Microsoft is doing to integrate its own upcoming goggle system, the HoloLens, with the existing Kinect motion-capture game controller. Through a Kinect interface, HoloLens users should be able to build up a virtual landscape simply by grabbing and manipulating stock elements, much like designers today manipulate a Photoshop image.

Of course, Microsoft is a big company and HoloLens is only a small piece of that stock's puzzle. Many of the best pure plays when it comes to either VR development or playback are either still privately held or have been absorbed into much larger technology conglomerates. For now, unless you want to accept that any virtual company you can invest in today will be 99 percent real with only a slice of pure, computer-generated reality behind it, options are limited. We'll simply have to be patient and wait for the right opportunity to emerge.

That lesson is part of the delicate balancing act of investing in public companies with the goal of disruptive innovation in mind. The truly transformational plays are still speculative. They exist largely in the future, when they exist at all—remember, somewhere between 75 and 90 percent of a typical early-stage venture capital portfolio will fizzle out on the way to the exit.

The IPO market will reject most companies at that stage as too small to ever grow into their deal valuations. The key is to keep our eyes on the ones that somehow make it through the window without being acquired along the way. If we can find a VR company some day at the right price, I'll be sure to let you know.

Google, famously, tried this with Google Glass. They were too early to market: people wearing Glass were derided as looking uncool, and there was not enough of a supporting ecosystem to make the benefits very clear. But let's imagine a world—and it's fast coming —where real-time intel on what you're looking at is just something everyone gets, and having it directly and discreetly overlaid on your field of vision is less intrusive than having to stop (or, more usually, continue moving with drastically diminished situational awareness) while staring down at your phone.

Obviously this can be used as an extension of the previous scenario. As you pass a business, an overlay will tell you that today pepperoni slices are buy-two-get-one-free at Frankie's Pizza, and Dexter Palmer will be signing his new novel at this particular Barnes & Noble on Saturday at noon. Obviously this is going to need some mediation lest your entire field of view be clogged with irrelevant ads, so your recommendation system would need to winnow notifications down for you. Since you haven't bought a book in ten years, there's no point in forwarding the bookstore notice to your eyeballs.

The New Economy Revolves around YOU

However, being given information when we want it (or, ideally, slightly before we want it) isn't the whole story. Not having to see things that make us uncomfortable is just as crucial. Tired of the panhandlers who line the route between where you park and your office? With augmented reality glasses and noise-cancelling earbuds, it will be possible for your devices to tell which of the people in your field of vision are likely to ask for money or otherwise irritate you and blur them out and cancel out the noises they make.

That ability to tune out the noise and follow your own voice makes this the best unintended consequence of all, giving you the latitude to operate according to your own priorities. You truly can become the disruptor here. In fact, the barriers to the citizen-disruptor are falling now as technology makes historical gatekeepers and intermediaries irrelevant.

Decades ago you needed a specialized broker to buy a house, another one to buy or sell every share of stock, and a travel agent with special credentials to get a plane ticket. Whole branches full of bankers gave you access to your money if you visited them at predetermined hours of the day. You probably followed orders from a corporate boss in a clear chain of command. When you found a new job, it was often because a professional recruiter got your name and got the process rolling.

Today you can do it all with a few swipes on your phone. Your profile in the world of 2050 is as large as you want it to be...as large as all the experts of the old economy stacked together. Start your own business. Be the retailer you want to see in the world. Be the job creator. Be the wealth creator. All that's required is the willpower to tune out the noise long enough to figure out how to do it yourself. I can't wait to see the future you build.

ABOUT
HILARY KRAMER

HILARY KRAMER is a fund manager, equity investor, and venture capitalist who has spent over thirty years as an investment trailblazer and highly respected stock market investor on Wall Street. The *Financial Times* calls her a "one-woman financial investment powerhouse" and the *Economist* distinguishes her as "one of the best-known investors in America."

A former analyst and investment banker at Morgan Stanley and Lehman Brothers, Ms. Kramer founded and ran a long-short hedge fund and has been chief investment officer overseeing more than $5 billion of debt and equity portfolios. A globally recognized futurist, she provides stock analysis and investment advice to her subscribers in her *GameChangers* newsletter from Eagle Financial Publications and to her listeners on *Kramer's Millionaire Maker*, a nationally syndicated radio show on the Salem Network. A certified fraud examiner, she has testified as an expert in investment suitability, portfolio construction, risk management, executive compensation, and corporate governance. She is a frequent guest TV and radio commentator on CNBC, CBS, Fox News, PBS, Reuters, and Bloomberg. Her editorials and commentaries have appeared in the *Wall Street Journal*, MarketWatch, CNBC.com, FoxNews.com, and *Forbes*.

Ms. Kramer was a founding member of the *Wall Street Journal* Women in Business board along with Christine Lagarde, president of the European Central Bank. Ms. Kramer has developed and taught numerous seminars over the years on risk management, alternative investments, equity investing and the global economy. She is a frequent speaker for professional organizations such as 100 Women in Hedge Funds, the National Association of Professional Women (NAPW), Tiger 21, the CFA Institute, the Council for European Investment Security (CEIS), and the Forbes Investor Advisory Institute. Ms. Kramer has also provided written and in-person testimony to the United States Senate regarding investment policy.

Ms. Kramer has served as a director to four publicly traded companies and is often asked to be a consultant to family offices and institutions, such as Montgomery Asset Management, Freddie Mac, and families on the Forbes list of global billionaires ranging from Latin America to the Middle East.

She remains an avid investor in emerging businesses and new technologies. Ms. Kramer was the initial investor in a cleantech venture capital fund in Colorado and serves on the board of directors as well as consults and invests in start-ups ranging from data-driven risk management to smart building technology to water treatment. In addition to her angel and venture investing, Ms. Kramer is also an activist investor in publicly traded equities representing investor rights in mergers & acquisitions. Ms. Kramer served as the co-head and board member of a $1 billion private equity fund jointly owned by Hicks, Muse that developed and invested in new programming content, as well as on the advisory board of numerous companies including today's leading international TV Satellite Company.

Ms. Kramer holds an MBA from the Wharton School of the University of Pennsylvania and a BS with honors from Wellesley College. She is the author of *Ahead of the Curve* (Simon & Schuster, 2007) and *The Little Book of Big Profits from Small Stocks* (Wiley, 2012).

INDEX